Purpose, Evolution
and the Mystery
of Life

Purpose, Evolution and the Mystery of Life

Proceedings of the Fourth
Annual Goshen Conference
on Religion and Science

John F. Haught
Healey Professor of Theology
Georgetown University

Edited by: Carl S. Helrich
Goshen College

Library and Archives Canada Cataloguing in Publication

Goshen Conference on Religion and Science (4th : 2004 : Goshen, Ind.)

Purpose, evolution and the mystery of life : proceedings of the Fourth Annual Goshen Conference on Religion and Science / John F. Haught ; edited by Carl S. Helrich.

Includes bibliographical references and index.
ISBN 1-894710-55-X

1. Religion and science--Congresses. I. Haught, John F. II. Helrich, Carl S. III. Title.

BL241.G68 2004   261.5'5   C2005-903536-6

PURPOSE, EVOLUTION AND THE MEANING OF LIFE: PROCEEDINGS OF THE FOURTH ANNUAL GOSHEN CONFERENCE ON RELIGION AND SCIENCE

Printed and bound at
Pandora Press
33 Kent Avenue
Kitchener, Ontario N2G 3R2
www.pandorapress.com
All rights reserved

International Standard Book Number: 1-894710-55-X

Contents

Editor's Preface

No one's thought is ever simple and no one's ideas can ever be summarized in short phrases. Even an outline is laden with nuances of interpretation and understanding. We can sometimes, however, express the basic tenets underlying our ideas in a very compact form and then develop them and explore the consequences with others. What can emerge is a deeper understanding on the part of all engaged. The annual Goshen Conference on Religion and Science is a forum for engaging, through lecture and discussion, the ideas of a single speaker active in the dialog between religion and science. The speaker for the 2004 conference was John F. Haught, Healey Professor of Theology at Georgetown University.

Professor Haught presented the elements of his thinking on cosmic purpose and evolution in three lectures illustrated by slides. In the discussion sessions participants explored these ideas through questions or comments. In some responses to probing questions Haught began by saying that he had come to this conference to find an answer to the question being asked. It is possible that the fundamental questions we ask do not change, but the answers change as we understand the questions more deeply. We must anticipate that we have never completed the journey.

Haught's thinking is, by his own admission, eclectic. He has blended the thoughts of others as a winemaker blends wines to bring out the nuances and sometimes hidden character of the sources. We encountered Whitehead, Teilhard, Tillich, Augustine and others in this blend. And Haught pointed to what he considered the primary messages of Christianity to help our thinking. What emerges points to a purposeful universe that embodies the restlessness that science teaches us is there and the Christian message of hope. The universe is not finished.

The image Haught placed before the conference was that of thirty volumes each with 450 pages. This set contained the story of the universe. Only the last eight volumes record the period during which there was life on earth. The dinosaurs are extinct on page 385 and self-consciousness appears on page 450 of volume thirty. We do not know how many pages are left to be written. And we do not know what those unwritten pages will reveal. But we do know that the story contained in those volumes is of a dynamic and not a static universe. In this image Haught pointed to the hope that is at the center of the Christian message. To find purpose in the universe is to blend this hope with the details of the emerging universe that science probes.

The scientific picture of the universe will always be materialistic. As Haught pointed out, when we seek a scientific understanding we choose to work in a framework that does not consider God. Science has been very successful in obtaining an understanding of the observable universe within the chosen framework. Haught well understands the scientific position and believes that the scientific approach to seeking understanding should be left alone. We should understand the scientific process, the picture this gives us, and appreciate that. However, we should not expect that this is the complete picture or that this is the only road to understanding. Evidence that our search should be broadened Haught found in simple examples such as the question posed to Socrates as to why he was sitting in prison. One answer may be physical and biological. But the deeper answer was in Socrates' belief that it was the correct and honorable thing to do. Any complete understanding of the universe must embrace Socrates' response.

Haught proposed that this understanding results in a layered explanation of what we observe. Scientific abstraction seeks simplicity leaving out many of the nuances we know are part of our understanding of daily life. The answer is not to return to the universe of Aristotle. But if we claim that a full understanding lies in any extreme then we miss what we are seeking. A more reasonable approach is to consider that any event has a number of explanations at differing levels none of which is false. Our understanding should embrace all.

As with each Goshen Conference we do not know where the speaker will lead us as the first evening begins to unfold. The reader can find this in the discussions printed here. Participation in this conference is an element of the adventure in understanding.

Carl S. Helrich
Goshen, 10 February, 2005

Lecture 1: Science and Cosmic Purpose

[Carl Helrich] Good evening, and welcome to the first public lecture of the fourth annual Goshen Conference on Religion and Science. I am delighted to see everyone of you and wish I could spend more time getting to know everybody. We have with us this evening Professor John F. Haught, from Georgetown University. Professor Haught is the Thomas Healey Distinguished Professor of Theology at Georgetown. This first lecture will be on "Science and Cosmic Purpose." Help me welcome Professor Haught.

[John Haught] Thank you very much, Carl. It's certainly an honor to be invited to this conference and have the opportunity to meet with some old friends as well as many new ones that I hope to make over the next few days. Thank you all very much for coming.

Well, as you know, for many years my main interest has been the relationship of science to religion. But I think that when you cut through all the specific questions that surround this topic, and when you get right down to the bottom of it, the fundamental issue is whether one can speak plausibly today of the universe as having some point, purpose or meaning to it. Now, a lot of you might be wondering why we should talk about this question at all. People are usually interested in the question of purpose or meaning in their own lives. But why should it be a concern to us as human beings whether or not the universe as a whole has any point or meaning to it?

Here's one way to look at it. Anybody who knows anything about modern science, biology, evolution, cosmology and physics has probably come to realize how intricately each one of us is tied into the whole universe. We are inseparable from it. And so I agree with the American philosopher W. T. Stace, who wrote back in 1942, in an article in *The Atlantic Monthly*, that if the whole scheme of things—meaning the whole cosmos—is pointless, then so also are our individual lives. Again, not everybody would agree with that, but I was delighted to see that Vaclav Havel, the outgoing president of the Czech Republic, in several speeches while he was still president, said this: "The crisis of the much needed global responsibility [and he's speaking here especially about ecological responsibility] is due to the fact that we've lost the sense that the universe has a purpose."[1] And if you poll the religions of the world, they would agree, almost unanimously, that it's important, especially for the sake of sustaining moral aspiration from generation to generation, that people believe that the universe is here for a reason.

However, we live in an age of science, and for many people today, especially in the intellectual world, the question is: Can we reconcile the ageless religious belief that the universe is here for a reason with what the natural sciences are saying? I'm sure that many of you are familiar with the famous quote from Steven Weinberg's book *The First Three Minutes* in which he says that "the more [scientifically] comprehensible the universe has become, the more pointless it also seems."[2] Perhaps less familiar is a similar quotation from Richard Feynman, another widely respected 20th century physicist, who said, "The great accumulation of understanding as to how the physical world behaves, only convinces one that this behavior has a kind of meaninglessness about it."[3]

Now compare these statements to what we might call the "Wisdom of the Ages," the great philosophical and religious traditions of humanity. Almost all of these thought of the universe as purposeful. What made it possible for traditional religions and philosophies to think of the cosmos as purposeful was that most of them had something like a hierarchical way of organizing the universe. The universe consisted of a ladder of levels, moving from matter at the bottom up through plant life, animal life, human consciousness, and sometimes intermediary realms of angelic beings, to Ultimate Reality and Meaning at the top. Each level could receive its meaning by being taken up into a higher level, and that level into an even higher, until ultimately all are assumed into the life of God.

This scheme operates according to what I like to call the "hierarchical principle." This principle maintains that a higher level in any hierarchy can encompass or comprehend a lower, but a lower cannot comprehend or encompass the higher. And so, what this principle would mean for our understanding of science and religion today, is that achieving cognitive competency at the lower levels does not necessarily qualify one to say anything about, or comment on, the higher levels. Almost unanimously, the great religions and philosophies thought that in order for us humans to be able to say anything about the higher levels, we would have to go through a process of personal transformation. Philosophy for many centuries required a discipline, an apprenticeship, or a set of exercises, allowing one to achieve *adaequatio*, that is, adequacy or competency. As E. F. Schumacher writes in *A Guide for the Perplexed*, one must achieve *adaequatio* in order to be in a position to comment on whether the higher levels exist at all, or on what their nature might be. The Wisdom of the Ages teaches that the more important something is, the more elusive it is to human consciousness. And so, if there is an ultimate meaning or purpose to the universe, it would lie, by definition, beyond the comprehension of human consciousness. If there is an ultimate meaning it might comprehend us and our consciousness, but our consciousness could not comprehend, or wrap itself around, it. This is the hierarchical principle.[4]

This doesn't mean, of course, that the ultimate level is unknowable in every sense. For we could have an awareness of being grasped by the ultimate. The theologian Paul Tillich defined faith as *the state of being grasped* by what we take to be of ultimate concern. But we can never attain a grasping or comprehending understanding of any conceivable ultimate meaning. Absolute clarity would actually diminish our sense of the ultimate. So if there is any purpose to the universe, we could refer to it only by way of symbols, metaphors and analogies. We could not justifiably pretend ever to have a clear and distinct understanding of what the purpose of things is.

Now compare this classical religious outlook to the contemporary scientific picture of the universe. The cosmos as portrayed by modern science is said, by the latest estimates, to be about 13.7 billion years old. You may picture the unfolding of the cosmic story in the following way. Imagine that you have thirty large books on your shelf, and each of those volumes is 450 pages long. Each page in each book stands for one million years. The Big Bang takes place on page one of Volume 1. But you'll notice that the first twenty-two tomes consist of what seems from the scientific perspective to be essentially lifeless and mindless physical stuff. The earth's story begins in Volume 21, four billion years ago. About a billion or so years later, in volume 22, the first sparks of life begin to flame up — about 3.8 billion years ago. But life is not in a hurry to become terribly complex until around the end of Volume 29, where the famous Cambrian Explosion takes place. All of a sudden the forms of life become much more complex and more interesting, at least from a human point of view. Even so, dinosaurs don't come in until after the middle of volume 30; and they go extinct on page 385, 65 pages from the end.

The last 65 pages comprise the age of mammals, and eventually primates and humans. Our hominid ancestors arrive on the last several pages of volume 30. But modern humans don't appear until possibly the last fifth or so of the very last page of Volume 30. That's when intelligence, ethical aspiration and other features we associate with our humanity burst onto the cosmic scene.

Now, if you're scientifically educated today, you can't help asking: What is the point of this great epic? Is there some continuous thread that ties together what is going on in Volume 1 with what's going on on page 450 of Volume 30? It doesn't seem so, at least to many scientific thinkers. It appears instead that there's a kind of aimlessness to the process. In asking whether there is a point to the universe, I think it's important to look for some kind of narrative continuity that would tie the 30 volumes together into some sort of meaningful whole. But it may be hard to find such coherence.

Notice that the hierarchical cosmology that provided the backbone of traditional spirituality and the sense of purpose apparently gets flattened out by contemporary science—horizontalized, you might say. Life seems hard to distinguish from lifeless matter. In the new cosmic story, life emerges only gradually out of lifeless matter.

And mind comes in apparently as a kind of cosmic afterthought. Finally, meaning, which was the highest level in the traditional hierarchy, seems — at least to modern and postmodern thought—to be nothing more than an illusion projected by the human mind onto the coldness of an impersonal cosmos.

As if the flattening of the hierarchy were not enough to squeeze purposiveness out of nature altogether, the ancient sense of reality has also been pulverized by another major development in modern thought. *Atomism*, the method of explaining complex things by breaking them down into their constituent particulars, has served to fragment the classic worldview into elemental pieces having no permanent significance. Atomism is an ancient temptation, associated especially with the pre-Socratic philosopher Democritus who said that all one needs to understand reality are two concepts, atoms and the void. Democritean atomism went underground for a number of centuries because of the dominance of Platonism and Aristotelian thought, both of which gave to "form" or pattern an importance that atomism did not permit. But in modern times, especially with the birth of classical physics in the 17th century, and particularly with the particles-in-motion universe of Newton, atomism returned with a vengeance. And by the time the 19th century came along and Darwinian theory burst onto the scene, it became possible — as is true even to this day — for many scientific thinkers to interpret evolution simply as a kind of reshuffling of the atomic elements that are said to make up the universe. This is the thrust of Daniel Dennett's book *Darwin's Dangerous Idea* (1995), for example. In the 1950s atomism received a significant boost by way of the developments in molecular biology, which tries as far as possible to explain life and mind in terms of chains of atoms. And even more recently atomism found a new partner in sociobiology, associated with E.O. Wilson and the derivative fields of evolutionary anthropology and evolutionary psychology, which try to explain human behavior in terms of the drive of genes (segments of DNA being the new atomic units) to get into the next generation.

Atomism, however, may be either a method or a philosophy. Methodological atomism, if I may call it that, is essential to science. Neuroscience, for example, rightly tries to explain mind as much as possible in terms of its atomic, molecular, cellular and modular constituents. But a more philosophical atomism has also appeared in modern times, claiming that all things are ontologically reducible to atomic particulars. It has done so in the shadow of the modern Cartesian expulsion of mind from matter. Mind, according to Descartes and his followers lies on one side of a sharp divide, and "matter" falls on the other. What this dualism has come to imply is that matter is *essentially mindless*. And once mind has thereby been exorcised from the realm of matter, this leaves only an atomized, mindless, and hence essentially purposeless, universe. It is on this imaginary universe of mindless stuff that modern cosmic pessimism has been confidently erected. Then, as if to add salt to the wound, beginning in the 19th century life's evolution has often come to be thought of as simply the reshuffling of atoms in organisms over the course of time. Life itself therefore has been assimilated into the pointless atomistic universe of modern cosmic pessimism. And by emphasizing the randomness, competitive struggle, and impersonality in life's evolution, Darwinian biology seems to many modern scientific thinkers to confirm the idea, once and for all, that we live in an essentially pointless universe. This cosmic pessimism is taken for granted in many popular scientific writings today, as well as in academic philosophy.

Can science detect purpose?

So in view of this purpose-denying cosmic pessimism is it intellectually plausible to maintain, along with our religious traditions, that there is anything of permanent significance going on in the universe? And can one make a case for cosmic purpose in a way that is consistent with science?

Before giving my own response to this question, let me look briefly at how classical theological traditions might deal with this large question. Their response is varied, but it is important to note that after religions became literate their theologies often compared the universe to a book. The book, in other words, became a model or analogy for the cosmos itself. What is important about a book is that it can be read at many different levels, and with varying degrees of *adaequatio*. Take, for example, Herman Melville's novel *Moby Dick*.[5] Suppose this book is lying on the floor of your house, and a monkey comes along and opens it up. What will the monkey see? Black marks on white pages. Is the monkey wrong? No, but the book *can* mean more. Then take a child who has just learned the letters of the alpha-

bet, and who opens up the same book. The novel, at the child's reading level, is a treasury of letters of a code. Again the child is not
wrong, but the book can still mean more. Suppose then an adoles-
cent reads the novel *Moby Dick* and writes a book report on it. The
report will likely outline the narrative accurately, but it will probably not provide a profound understanding of the mind of Melville.
Finally an adult, someone weathered by the storms of life, picks up
the same novel. Having undergone a process of personal transformation, and having attained a deeper degree of *adaequatio*, this reader
will be able to see things in the great classic that the others had missed
completely.

Classical theological understanding would allow that the cosmos is something like a book, and that it can therefore be read at
different levels. Science — for example physics and chemistry —
can read the universe in such a way as to decipher its alphabet and
grammar, but the universe can still mean more. Maybe there are
deeper levels of meaning in the universe that science itself does not
have the *adaequatio* to say anything about. Science, after all, is not
wired to detect any signals of purpose, and so it would not be surprising if science failed to say anything one way or the other about
purpose in the universe. From the time of its origins at the beginning of the modern period, physics and the other sciences have approached the natural world without any formal concern about meaning, purpose, value, subjectivity, intentionality or God. What science finds out about nature may have implications for how philosophers and theologians answer the question of purpose, but by definition science refrains from speaking about purpose itself. If scientists insist on holding forth on the question of cosmic purpose, they
do so not as scientists, but as philosophers.

And yet today a lot of scientists would say that times have
changed. Maybe science can be more directly helpful in answering
the question of cosmic purpose than we thought possible earlier.
The physics of the early universe, some scientists and philosophers
are now proposing, has made it possible to rethink the whole question of cosmic purpose. This approach begins with the undeniable
fact that we all have minds. But how did we come to have minds?
Science tells us that it's because our brains have evolved to a degree
of complexity sufficient to allow the leap into thought to take place.
But of course science also tells us that we would not have these brains

without evolution. Over a several million-year period the primate brains of our ancestors became physically complicated to the point where (modern human) minds could emerge. However, evolution itself presupposes the existence of life, and there can be no life without planets endowed with just the right chemical makeup to give rise to and sustain life. The existence of life, in turn, requires carbon and heavier elements in the chemical chart. But, again, we can't take carbon for granted since it was not always available in the universe. So how did it get there? Through an extremely complicated, but now well understood, physical process hydrogen and helium were turned into carbon in the enormous heat of massive stars. Then during supernova explosions, carbon and other elements essential for life were distributed through space. Subsequently this detritus was compacted by the force of gravity into secondary and tertiary solar systems such as our own.

But, then, we can't take these massive stars for granted either. Astrophysicists now realize that in order for these stars to exist the universe's expansion rate and its gravitational coupling constant had to have been given almost precisely the values that they have. Otherwise the massive stellar ovens that cook up carbon would never have formed. The rate of cosmic expansion, the force of gravity and other coincidences had to have been "fine-tuned" in order to bring about life and mind. So the existence of life and mind, as it now turns out, is exquisitely sensitive to conditions and constants that fell into place at the time of the Big Bang. And the precision characteristic of the primordial suite of cosmic characteristics suggests to some scientists that the conditions for mind were front-loaded into the universe, from the very first microsecond of its existence.

So is it possible that astrophysics itself has uncovered a kind of directional purposiveness in the universe? If there is going to be a purposeful universe, it would seem that there has to be at least some kind of directionality to it. The universe has to be more than just aimlessly meandering around. And hasn't science found the necessary directionality: in the universe's aim toward bringing about minds?

If you don't want to go that far, it seems to me that you at least have to admit that it is no longer plausible to say that mind is only accidentally related to the rest of the universe. You may still conjecture that the fine-tuned universe itself is an unlikely statistical accident in the play of large numbers within the framework of a multiverse (as does the astronomer Martin Rees). But it seems to me that in the light of physics today the existence of mind is no accident within the framework of our own Big Bang cosmos. And what this implies, at least as far as modern thought is concerned, is that the dichotomy that Descartes and his followers drew between mind and matter — such that matter came to be thought of as essentially mindless — is wiped out. The boundary between mind and matter is much more fluid than we formerly thought, and so it does not seem appropriate to hold any longer that we live in an *essentially* mindless universe. And, if the universe is in some way intrinsically mental, then it could be receptive, at least in principle, to the implantation of a pervasive meaning. On the other hand, if the universe were essentially mindless, there is no way in which purpose or meaning could settle into it as an inherent feature of things. To go back to our thirty volumes, then, hasn't science itself, independently of theology and religion, found an essential connection, a narrative thread, that ties page one of Volume 1 to the last page of Volume 30? Can't we say, at the very least, that purpose in the universe consists of an orientation toward life and mind?

But is the universe purposeful?

I should pause here and define more carefully what I mean by purpose. Purpose quite simply means the realization of a value. Any process that seems to be aiming toward or bringing about what is self-evidently good or valuable may be called purposive. We know from personal experience that what ties together the moments of our own lives, insofar as we think of our lives as meaningful, is the sense that somehow we are actualizing, or helping to bring about, something of permanent value. Couldn't it be said, then, that any universe which is in the process of realizing *mind*, an undeniable value, is at the very least a purposive one?

Well, some people would accept that idea, but others think we are in danger of defining mind here entirely too narrowly, entirely too terrestrially and anthropocentrically. If we are going to talk about the *whole* cosmos, maybe we should be looking for something wider than mind—at least as we humans usually understand the term. One notable scientist and religious thinker who has sought a wider-than-human understanding—and who did it many years before any of us here got involved in the study of science and religion—was Pierre Teilhard de Chardin (1881-1955). Teilhard was a Jesuit priest as well as a geologist and paleontologist. While he was doing his studies, he developed a deep sense of the evolutionary character of life and the universe as a whole, and he began to write essays integrating his own Christian faith into an understanding of evolution and the larger universe. His religious superiors, having become quite alarmed at some of his ideas, sent him to China where he became one of the main geologists of the Asian continent. As a geologist he never had any trouble gaining the respect of his scientific friends and peers, but he was not permitted to publish his essays on religion and science. He died in New York, virtually unknown, on Easter Sunday in 1955, and only several Jesuits accompanied him to his burial in Poughkeepsie, New York. It was only after he died that his central publications became available, and Teilhard rapidly became one of the most important religious thinkers of the 20th century.

If the universe is to have a purpose, Teilhard argued, it has to have at least a loose kind of directionality to it. In other words, it has to be more than just aimlessly wandering around. And if anybody looks carefully at the evolution of life in the context of the whole cosmic unfolding, it is not hard to see that there clearly is an axis of directionality running through it. Moreover, this directionality is measurable. It consists of the gradual increase in organized physical complexity in the course of cosmic history. As atoms become molecules, molecules become cells and cells become organisms, the universe grows increasingly more complex in its organization. Then in the emergence of vertebrates, primates, and finally humans, nervous systems and brains become almost unimaginably complex.[6]

Furthermore, there is no reason to insist that evolution has now come anywhere near the end of its journey. If you look under your feet, behind your back and over your head, you will see a new type of organized physical complexity now taking shape. Teilhard calls this latest evolutionary level of being the "noosphere," from the Greek word *nous*, which means "mind." The human phenomenon is now weaving itself collectively around our planet, taking advantage of politics, economics, education, scientific developments and especially communication technology. Teilhard, incidentally, is sometimes called the "prophet of the Internet" because he predicted that through technological complexification the earth would continue to clothe itself in something like a brain.

This is the noosphere. It is all so new that science still doesn't yet know quite what to make of it. In evolution, after all, things take millions and millions of years, but the formation of the noosphere so far is a matter of only thousands, and, in its latest stages, especially of the last 200 years. So we should not assume that the universe's aim toward more and more complex physical developments is at its end. Perhaps, for all we know, evolutionary creation is still at the cosmic dawn.[7]

Nevertheless, physical complexification in evolution is interesting to Teilhard only because, in direct proportion to the gradual increase in organized physical complexity, there is a corresponding increase in *consciousness*. Teilhard refers here to the "law of complexity-consciousness," which maintains that consciousness increases in direct proportion to the degree of increase in physical complexity. What's going on in the universe, at the very least, is a gradual increase in the intensity of consciousness. And this is enough to fill it with purpose, a notion that I defined earlier as the "realization or actualization of a value." It is impossible to deny consistently that consciousness is a self-evident value, for if you find yourself denying it this can only be because you value your consciousness enough to make such a judgment. Since consciousness is clearly a value, a universe that is in the business of bringing about more and more intense versions of consciousness is a pretty interesting universe. It would not be rash to call it purposeful.

Not only is there an increase in complexity and consciousness, there is also an intensification of freedom. The aim toward freedom is another trend that makes it possible to call the universe meaningful. But the increase of consciousness and freedom occurs only because of a deeper tendency of cosmic reality to organize itself around a center. "Centration" in cosmic history is already going on at the level of the atom, where the nucleus somehow organizes the subatomic elements. And centration continues at the level of the eukaryotic living cell with its well-defined nucleus. Centration becomes much more intense at the level of vertebrates with their complex central nervous systems. In primates centration intensifies further in the heightened consciousness made possible by a more complex brain. Then with humans centration reaches the form of self-awareness. Teilhard's point is that, by anybody's standards, in evolution there has been a discernible directional increase in centration and, along with it, an intensifying of inwardness or subjectivity.[8]

And now that the universe has reached the stage of the noosphere, what is the form that the search for the center takes? It takes many forms, but the most characteristic way in which the search for the center — which has always been going on in the universe — continues is that of *religion*. Religion fits into the evolutionary universe as the way in which conscious life carries on the search for a Center. Religion can be defined as the "way to the Center," and that is how Teilhard understood it. All religions have the tendency to seek a higher reality or a Super-center, as he called it. And of course for Teilhard, who was a Christian theist, the name of this Supercenter is God. Teilhard understood God as having become incarnate in the Christ, and he understood Christ as the physical goal of cosmic evolution. But in all of religion a search for the Center has been going on from the time of the earliest expressions of spiritual inquiry. Consequently, we should look at religion not only theologically, historically, psychologically or sociologically, but also cosmologically. For Teilhard religion is the way in which the *universe*, now that it has reached the level of self-awareness, continues its ageless search for the Center. So religion, instead of being opposed to evolution, is absolutely essential to its future.

As Teilhard writes in his book *Activation of Energy*:

> What is most vitally necessary to the thinking earth is a faith and a great faith and ever more faith, to know that we are not prisoners, to know that there is a way out, that there is air and light and love somewhere beyond the reach of all death. To know this, to know that it is neither an illusion nor a fairytale, that if we are not to perish smothered in the very stuff of our being—this is what we must at all costs secure. And it is there that we find what I may well be so bold as to call the evolutionary role of religions.[9]

For the sake of the universe and its future we must cultivate and purify, not abandon, our religious traditions.

Finally, for Teilhard, the meaning of our own lives must also have something to do with our participation in the evolutionary process of complexification, socialization, centration — of searching for deeper freedom and increasing consciousness. Participating in evolution is often difficult and painful. But suffering and struggle, about which I will speak in the following lecture, are for Teilhard best understood as the dark side of an unfinished universe. Obviously suffering is much more than that, but that is how it would fit into an evolving and still unperfected cosmos. Teilhard believes that in the end the struggle will all have proven to be worth the effort. But for anything significant to come of evolution, henceforth each of us has to make some serious choices in our lives. He calls this set of choices the "Grand Option."[10]

First of all we have to decide between whether we want to live as pessimists or as optimists. If we choose the path of pessimism, including what I have been calling cosmic pessimism, this can only lead to an evolutionary dead end. Evolution on earth will terminate tragically if we fall into a state of despair or pessimism about the future. But suppose you choose to live for the future? Suppose the horizon opens up ahead of you? Then you still have to make a choice as to what kind of future you are going to hope for. One option is to aspire to get out of this world altogether. You may find this option presented abundantly in traditional Christian spirituality. Teilhard refers to this option as the "optimism of withdrawal." It is a hope to get out of the mess we are in here, to leave the universe and the earth behind as soon as possible, so that we can find our true destiny elsewhere.

This is a very attractive and comforting option for millions of people. However, another horizon of hope has opened up because of science, and especially the arrival of evolutionary thought and new developments in cosmology. This alternative prospect is the "optimism of evolution." It is based on the sense that the universe is still not finished, still in the process of being created. So why should we not get excited about participating in the ongoing creation of this universe? The universe may still have a great future ahead of it. Teilhard urges his fellow believers, as well as people in general, to follow this path of ongoing creative evolution. It will not lead you away from God, he said, but more fully into the heart of the God who wills to share with you the process of creation.

However, if you take the path of evolution, if you see the future opening up before you, you still have to make a choice between whether you want to evolve on your own or in communion with others. With the emphasis on individualism in modern times it is a very strong temptation to go it alone. But individualism is ultimately an evolutionary dead end also. It is only by way of the path of communion, of joining cooperatively with others, that evolution advances. And you do not need to fear that this joining with others is going to rob you of your individuality. In fact you are going to find your true and unique selfhood only by engaging along with others in "a great hope held in common."[11] There is a fundamental principle in evolution and in the nature of reality as such: *true union differentiates.* True union does not homogenize, does not reduce to uniformity. True union paradoxically lets the other be, and it lets the components of the more comprehensive unity achieve their freedom, their individuality, their independence.[12]

Now how do we know this? We know this because if we look at the way evolution has worked in the past, we can see that it has moved from one level to the other only by passing recurrently through three phases: the phase of *divergence*, followed by *convergence*, followed by *emergence*. I cannot go into detail with each phase, but let me exemplify the point by reference to living cells. As individual cells (single-celled forms of life) began to inhabit this planet, they spent — as we now know — a couple billion years simply spreading out over the face of the globe. This was the phase of divergence. But at a certain point in the past, a critical threshold was passed, and then the phase of convergence began to occur: the cells began to coagulate, first in looser associations, but then in tighter and more integrated forms of communion. That was the phase of convergence. Finally, at the point of very intense convergence, the emergence of something new, namely, multi-celled, self-integrated organisms occurred.

So the pattern, once again, is: divergence, followed by convergence, followed by emergence. And this same pattern has repeated itself at various stages of matter's complexification. Now let us move to the latest dominant phase in evolution, when humans came onto the scene. Our species spent more than the first 100,000 years of its existence on this planet spreading out or diverging in tribal patterns of existence. Then about five to eight thousand years ago, in places like the Nile River basin and Mesopotamia, the individual human cells and tribes began to converge more tightly onto one another, first in the ancient city-states but more recently in the nation-states and even more recently in what Teilhard began to call planetization. If we look at what has been happening historically, politically, economically and technologically, especially in communications, it would seem that we are going through a very tight type of convergence process now. For all we know, we are just now passing the threshold from divergence to convergence — in an ambiguous and uncertain way. Now we have to imagine what life on earth will be like, psychically speaking, Teilhard says, a million years from now, keeping in mind that a million years is not very long in evolution. So we should not give up on ourselves. We are still very new to evolution. Is it even possible that something new and great is emerging through us?[13]

Teilhard was a Christian, and he had read the letters of St. Paul very carefully. He took seriously Paul's sense that the whole universe was straining for new creation, that the body of Christ was forming out of many members and that it extended out to the whole universe. This Pauline vision was one that Teilhard wanted to transplant into the evolutionary concepts of the 20th century. What he saw happening now on our planet reminded him of what had occurred a long time ago in evolution when the primate brain became sufficiently complicated for the leap into "thought" to take place. The law of complexity-consciousness — that consciousness, and therefore intensity of being, corresponds to the degree of organized physical complexity — permeates everything that Teilhard writes. And now we can see that a complexification process like that of the brain's evolution is occurring on a planetary scale: the earth is weaving around itself something analogous to a brain. If the parallelism is instructive, why shouldn't we anticipate that something momentous is afoot on this earth and, as I'll show in a moment, possibly elsewhere in the universe as well. Isn't it possible that something new and unimaginably complex is still being created? And don't we almost have an obligation to participate in that adventure of creation?[14]

But now let us take these reflections even further and reflect on the possibility of intelligent life elsewhere in the universe. I think that if he were here today Teilhard would probably pay even more attention to this topic than in the few scattered allusions he did make to it. I believe that Teilhard's thought could be extended in an age of SETI (The Search for Extraterrestrial Intelligence) in the following way. [15]

Let us start with what we know. We know that throughout the universe there has been a gradual increase in organized physical complexity, starting with pre-atomic matter, then moving on to atoms, molecules and what Christian de Duve, the French biologist, has called "vital dust," referring to the carbon compounds that make up as much as 40% of interstellar dust. We know without a doubt that the complexification process has advanced at least this far throughout the cosmos. We also know that at least on earth the process of complexifying matter has gone even further. Out of the vital dust have emerged cells, organisms, vertebrates, primates and humans. And now the noosphere is beginning to take on an even more complex shape on a planetary scale. Who knows what else might emerge beyond that?

Now, according to Teilhard, we also know that in direct proportion to the increase in organized physical complexity, on our planet at least, there has arisen a corresponding increase in consciousness. So don't we have here a framework of inquiry, a heuristic perhaps, in terms of which we could make cosmic and theological sense of extraterrestrial intelligent life if we were ever to encounter it? Teilhard was experimenting only gingerly with such ideas during his life. But on the basis of his general understanding of evolution isn't it possible that if extraterrestrial intelligence turns out to be plentiful, then something like extraterrestrial noospheres are also in the process of being created? If this turns out to be the case, then these individual noospheres would become the cells, the atoms, the fundamental units, of an unimaginable cosmic extension of consciousness. We don't yet know how this would be possible, since the noospheres would have to communicate with one another if a new phase of convergence is to occur. And, no doubt, these speculations will sound too wild for most people. But at least Teilhard provides an intelligible framework for thinking about such possibilities in the context of a purposeful universe.

So let me go back now to the question I asked earlier: can cosmic purpose be an intelligible idea in an age of science? Human religious sensibilities were first shaped in terms of a pre-scientific, vertical hierarchy of being. Even to this day the spiritual lives of most of us, including scientists, have been molded by traditions that arose long before we had any sense of an evolving universe. How then can we map the vertical hierarchy of classic theology and philosophy onto the 30-volume, horizontal unfolding of life, mind and meaning out of lifeless and mindless matter?

Teilhard's answer to that question is not terribly complicated. First of all, think of God as "up ahead," and not just up above. In fact, this is a very biblical way of thinking about God. The God of the Bible is the God who comes from the future, and urges or encourages the people of God to move toward the fulfillment that lies only in the future. The God of Abraham, the God of promise, draws the world toward unity from up ahead. Second, think of the cosmic hierarchy not as a vertical but an *emergent* hierarchy, one in which matter historically prepares the way for the appearance life, life for mind, and mind for spirit. It is not so difficult, after all, as Teilhard himself proposed, to connect the great traditions—what I have been calling the Wisdom of the Ages—with the evolutionary world view. Just rearrange the religious furniture in your mind a little. Think of the world not so much as leaning on the past, and don't think of creation as something that takes place exclusively in the past, but think of the world as always "leaning on the future," a future which for Teilhard is ultimately nothing other than God. God is the world's Future, and it is as Future that God is the world's ultimate support.[16] In this reconfiguration it is not inconceivable that the vine of religious meaning that traditionally wove itself around the vertical hierarchical lattice-work can now be rewound around the horizontal-evolutionary picture of a still unfinished creation.

Whitehead and Cosmic Purpose

Teilhard's proposals, I believe, are still powerfully relevant to the question of cosmic purpose. Let me conclude, however, with what may be an even wider cosmic vision. It is proposed by the great philosopher and mathematician Alfred North Whitehead. Whitehead is not somebody philosophers talk about much these days. This is unfortunate. Theologians refer to him much more often than philosophers do. Who was he? Whitehead was a widely-read, deeply-learned intellectual who taught mathematics at Cambridge University and then later in London. When he was about to retire from a lifetime of teaching, Harvard University invited him to come to Cambridge in the United States. He accepted the invitation and took up the post of University Professor at Harvard where he rapidly became one of America's great philosophers. After coming to the

United States he increasingly talked about science and religion, stating that the future of civilization hangs on their getting along with each other.[17]

In his book *Adventures of Ideas* Whitehead talks very explicitly about what he considered to be the fundamental aim or purpose of the universe. The purpose of the universe, as he saw it, is to bring about more and more intense versions of *beauty*. Now beauty, like consciousness, is an immediately self-evident value. We find great beauty irresistible and allow ourselves to be carried away by it. So much do we value it that we cannot help being captured by it. Keeping in mind the definition of purpose I gave earlier—the actualizing of value—any process that is in the business of bringing about more and more intense versions of beauty, which for Whitehead is the greatest of values, could be called, at least in a loose sense, teleological or purposive. The universe is at bottom just such a process.[18]

What Whitehead means by beauty is the synthesis of novelty on the one hand and order on the other, a marriage of contrast on one side with harmony on the other.[19] If there is too much of one and not enough of the other then beauty is lacking. If there is too much novelty, and not enough order, there will be a tendency toward chaos. But if there is too much order and not enough novelty, or too much harmony without sufficiently sharp contrast, then the result will be monotony, a state of things that evokes the feeling of anesthesia rather than of peaceful enjoyment. Both chaos and monotony are ways in which the universe can move away from its central aim toward the instantiation of more intense beauty. The cosmic aim toward beauty, therefore, is always risky. There can at times and places be too much novelty or too much order, too much chaos or too much monotony. These are forms of *evil* that call out for redemption by a wider and deeper beauty. Whitehead called the cosmos an "adventure" because the risk of evil is always present. Anything purposive has great peril attached to it.[20]

It is from science that we have learned that the cosmos has always been restless for adventure, that it has generally aimed toward more and more intense versions of ordered novelty. Our great traditions, the Wisdom of the Ages, knew nothing about this fundamental adventurousness of the physical world itself. But we've learned from the sciences that we live in a restless universe, and so somehow theology and religious thought have to come to grips with that fact. Whitehead himself wanted to know why the universe is so restless. Not only the order but also the restlessness of nature required an *ultimate* explanation. If God is the ultimate source of order then God must also be the ultimate source of novelty as well. But this means that God is the ultimate reason why the universe doesn't just stand still. God is not just the upholder of the status quo, but also the disturber of the status quo. God is not interested only in order, but in more intense versions of order. God, in other words, is concerned that there be evolution.

A universe in process requires that there be available to it a reservoir of novel possibilities. And these possibilities have to be waiting somewhere. They do not simply come into the process from nowhere. Where they wait for the moment of relevant actualization, Whitehead surmised, is in God. God is the source of the novel possibilities that allow the universe to be a great adventure rather than a stagnant monotony. But God does not forcefully stamp new possibilities onto the cosmos. Rather, as befits the character of love — and here Whitehead takes seriously the religious notion that God is love—God acts persuasively rather than coercively. Love does not force. Love is not dictatorial. Love lets the other be. And insofar as love acts persuasively rather than coercively, God allows for a universe in which there is room for abundant disorder, accidents, and chaos, but also freedom. And I would like to add that only such a universe can allow for the kind of meandering and experimentation that we find in Darwinian evolution.

I will say more about Darwin in the following lecture, but you can gather here that biological evolution can dwell rather comfortably within a Whiteheadian vision of things. Keep in mind, however, that in all events God's will or God's purpose for the universe is the maximizing of beauty. This intensifying of beauty—which would surely be inclusive of what Teilhard calls consciousness—is what God wants. This also means that the universe, since it is not forcefully managed by an engineering deity, is likely to be one in which there is a great risk of evil. However, in Whitehead's view, there is also the possibility of redemption. Whitehead's God experiences everything that goes on in the universe, takes everything that happens in the world into the divine life.[21] And in ways that science itself cannot articulate, God orders the totality of things into a wider and increasingly more intense beauty. I like to view Whitehead's cosmos as configured primordially by an *aesthetic cosmological principle* as distinct from the *anthropic* cosmological principle. It seems to me that in the light of science we can speak quite plausibly about a universe that is ordered not so much by an initial design or plan, but by the *promise* of more and more intense versions of beauty.

Whitehead, I should add, also thinks of God not as standing aloof from the suffering of the world, but as taking the world's suffering into the divine life. God is a "fellow sufferer" who embraces the world's entire evolution. In the beauty of God's own experience the universe finds its everlasting redemption even though it will eventually experience some sort of physical "death." Thus, a universe that is oriented, even if not always successfully, toward bringing about more and more intense versions of beauty deserves to be called a purposeful one. And, finally, the meaning of our own lives in this Whiteheadian framework would consist, in part at least, of our own creative participation in the ongoing process of intensifying the beauty of the universe we live in.

Notes

[1] Vaclav Havel, *Civilization*, (April/May), 1998, 53.

[2] Steven Weinberg, *The First Three Minutes* (New York: Basic Books, 1977), 144

[3] Richard Feynman, *The Meaning of It All: Thoughts of a Citizen Scientist* (New York: Perseus Books, 1999), 32.

[4] See E. F. Schumacher, *A Guide for the Perplexed* (New York: Harper Colophon Books, 1978), 18ff.

[5] Here I am adapting an idea developed by E. F. Schumacher in *A Guide for the Perplexed*.

[6] For a fuller picture there is no substitute for reading Pierre Teilhard de Chardin, *The Human Phenomenon*, trans. by Sarah Appleton-Weber (Portland, Oregon: Sussex Academic Press), 1999.

[7] Pierre Teilhard de Chardin, *The Prayer of the Universe*, trans. by René Hague. (New York, Harper & Row, 1973), 120-21.

[8] See especially Teilhard de Chardin, *Activation of Energy*, trans. René Hague (New York: Harcourt Brace Jovonovich 1970), 97-128.

[9] Ibid., 238.

[10] Teilhard de Chardin, *The Future of Man*, trans. by Norman Denny (New York: Harper Colophon Books, 1969), 39-63.

[11] Ibid. 75.

[12] Teilhard, *Activation of Energy*, 116.

[13] See, for example, Teilhard, *The Future of Man*, 64-84; 129-44; 255-71.

[14] Ibid.

[15] Teilhard, *Activation of Energy*, 126-27.

[16] Ibid. 239.

[17] Alfred North Whitehead, *Science and the Modern World* (New York: The Free Press, 1967), 181-82.

[18] Alfred North Whitehead, *Adventures of Ideas* (New York: The Free Press, 1967), 252-96; Alfred North Whitehead, *Process and Reality,* corrected edition, ed. by David Ray Griffin and Donald W. Sherburne (New York: The Free Press, 1978), 62, 183-85, 255 and *passim*; Alfred North Whitehead, *Modes of Thought* (New York: The Free Press, 1968), 8-104. See also Charles Hartshorne, *Man's Vision of God* (Chicago and New York: Willett, Clark & Company, 1941), 212-29.

[19] Whitehead, *Adventures of Ideas* (New York: The Free Press, 1967), 265.

[20] Ibid. 252-96.

[21] For this and many other features of Whitehead's religious vision see John B. Cobb, Jr. and David Griffin, *Process Theology: an Introductory Exposition* (Philadelphia: Westminster Press, 1976), 123-24.

Lecture 2: Darwin and Divine Providence

As most people know, the religious world in general and the Christian world in particular have had a tough time coming to grips with the rather ragged Darwinian picture of life. For many theists today, reconciling the idea of God with evolution remains as difficult as it was immediately after Darwin wrote *On The Origin of Species*. Christians and Muslims in particular have trouble reconciling Darwin's picture of the way life evolves with the consoling doctrine of divine providence. The word "providence" comes from the word provide, and the Darwinian recipe for evolution—random events, impersonal natural selection and an enormous span of (deep) time—seems to contradict the belief that God really provides for the world, for life in general, and especially for people within the world.

In order to grasp the significance of the Darwinian picture of life, it is good to remember that the doctrine of providence came into our religious awareness long before people had any sense of biological evolution and an expanding universe. The doctrine of providence, like that of purpose, had entwined itself around the static, vertical and hierarchical universe that I discussed in the previous lecture. This was a much more limited and manageable world than the one that science has given us beginning with Copernicus and Galileo. The classical, pre-scientific cosmos was structured in accordance with what Arthur Lovejoy and others have called The Great Chain of Being whose links are tied together but which are ontologically distinct. The discontinuity of levels in the hierarchy of being allowed humans to think of themselves as inhabiting a relatively high level in the whole scheme of things, and this elevated status gave them the confidence that they were cared for by divine providence in a very special way. The fact that evolution seems to wipe out the ancient sense of hierarchical discontinuity, therefore, is a major reason why it is still so unsettling for a lot of people to look closely at Darwin's portrait of life.

To dramatize this point, let us call to mind once again the new scientific picture of the universe that I discussed in the previous talk. We live in a 13.7 billion year old, expanding cosmos that is said to unfold only gradually, one in which life seems to have popped up as a kind of accident of chemistry and in which mind appeared only an instant ago. Picture the cosmic story as unfolding in thirty volumes consisting of 450 pages each, each page representing a million years of natural history. The first twenty-two volumes seem essentially lifeless and mindless. The earth story gets underway in Volume 21, and life begins in Volume 22. Once it emerges, life consists mostly of single cells, very simple at first and only gradually becoming more complex, until near the end of Volume 29. Here the Cambrian Explosion occurs, during which life becomes much more complex and multicellular. Even so, life takes its time. Dinosaurs don't appear until after the middle of Volume 30. And they die out 65 pages from the end of the book, making room for the age of mammals. Our hominid ancestors appear in the last several pages of the last book, and modern humans come onto the scene only near the bottom of the very last page.

What I want to focus on in this lecture is how to think of divine providence, given the evolutionary recipe for life. Once life comes about it hands itself over to the well-known Darwinian formula that consists of the three ingredients mentioned above: accidents, natural selection and an enormous amount of time. For many evolutionists this recipe seems to be enough to explain *ultimately* what's going on in life. There is no room for divine providence.

First the accidents: Accidents come in, for many Darwinians, first of all, in the spontaneous origin of life itself. And after life comes about, accidents appear plentifully in the random variations that today we call genetic mutations. These random variations provide the raw material for natural selection. Then, as Stephen Jay Gould and others have emphasized, accident (or "contingency," to use the philosophical term) comes into the picture in the many undirected events in natural history that cause life to evolve in unpredictable and unplanned ways. Take, for example, the meteorite impact that occurred in the Yucatan peninsula 65 million years ago, apparently wiping out the dinosaurs and opening up new niches for the development of mammalian life. What would life have been like if the meteorite had not crashed into the earth? Gould and many others think that the outcome would have been completely different from what it is. We humans, to cite one possibility, would not be here. Gould understands contingency, chance or accident to be fundamentally explanatory of what goes on in evolution.

Second, the Darwinian recipe includes the ingredient of lawful constraint, including the laws of physics, but also the *law* of natural selection. The blind and impersonal mechanism of selection allows only reproductively successful variations to survive while others are wiped out along the way. It discards all the rest in what seems to many religious believers to be a very unfair manner, allowing only certain "fit" organisms to survive and bear offspring. Third, Darwin's recipe takes the first two ingredients, accident and natural selection, and stirs them up in the bowl of deep cosmic time, the roughly four billion years of experimentation that evolution has had available to bring about all the diversity of life. For a lot of Darwinians today, this recipe seems sufficient to cook up every feature and every species of life. Nothing else seems necessary.

In the previous lecture I asked whether it is possible to map the spiritualities that took shape in the context of the classic, pre-evolutionary hierarchy onto our new scientific picture of an evolving, horizontally unfolding universe. Here, however, I want to focus on the question of divine providence that bothers many theists who have looked at Darwin's startling picture of life. After Darwin is the classic religious trust in divine providence a plausible idea at all?

Here are some possible responses:

1) The first is to assert that the doctrine of divine providence has become totally unbelievable. Many people in the scientific and philosophical communities today would stake everything on this claim.

In the religious community possibly as many as half of the Christians in America would agree that Darwinian evolution would be antithetical to belief in divine providence.

2) Others would suggest that before we rule out providence altogether after Darwin, we should consider placing the evolution of life within the larger context of the *whole* cosmic process. If we look at the wider picture of the universe now being put together by the many different sciences, especially astrophysics, maybe we can still allow for divine providence in the initial cosmic design and physical fine-tuning that would allow for the emergence and evolution of life later on in the story.

3) Another response, however, insists that the best way to approach our question of evolution and providence is simply to admit that we shall never be able to make any clear sense of the Darwinian recipe. For all we know, Darwin might be essentially correct, but behind the rough surface of life's evolution there may very well lurk a hidden, but splendid, divine plan for the universe and life, one in which each event has a preordained place and all wrinkles are ultimately ironed out in the mind of God. Appealing to the story of Job, this third approach would advise us to press our fingers to our lips and remain silent about things that are too big for us. This is a *fideistic* approach, that is, one that prescribes that we all make a pure leap of faith in the providence of God *in spite of* the absurdity that seems to be present in the universe, especially in evolution. It does not ask that we deny the truth of Darwin's theory, only that we confess that we cannot make any obvious theological sense of it. I know of a good many devout believers, in both the scientific and religious communities, who are most comfortable with this standpoint.

4) Other theists, however, are more theologically adventurous. They assert that we can at least try to understand what God might be up to in evolution. It may be possible to redeem the notion of divine providence in a scientific age, they suggest, if we interpret evolution as a kind of divine curriculum in which God allows life, and eventually human character, to develop or improve. Maybe we can legitimate Darwin theologically if we interpret evolution as divine pedagogy and earth as a "soul school."

5) A fifth proposal connects the unfinished character of the expanding universe and life's evolution even more directly to divine providence. Maybe God's care or divine providence is manifest pre-

cisely in the fact that the universe is still being created, with all the risk and tragedy that new creation inevitably brings with it. Teilhard de Chardin makes just this case and it deserves our careful attention.

6) If you are a follower of Alfred North Whitehead, you may be able to find hints of providence in the tragic beauty of an adventurous cosmic process that unfolds partly by way of the Darwinian route.

7) And finally — this will be my own way of approaching our topic — I wonder if it isn't possible to discover the presence of providence lurking deep down in the apparent abyss of Darwin's threefold recipe itself. Perhaps, in the randomness, lawful constraints and deep time that make evolution work, divine love is already making itself fully present to the life-story.

A Closer Look

What I shall do now is zoom in a bit more closely on each of these seven proposals. I'm not going to spend as much time on some as on others, but I think each deserves further examination.

1) It is the conviction of many scientists today, especially those familiar with biology, that the Darwinian understanding of evolution has made the idea of providence completely unbelievable. It is hard to look at the apparent struggle, pain, warfare and brutality in evolution, especially of life feeding on life, without asking where divine providence is in this apparently uncaring process? Charles Darwin himself, in a letter to one of his friends exclaimed: "What a book a devil's chaplain might write on the clumsy, wasteful, blundering, low and horridly cruel works of nature," and he referred to what he called "the dreadful but quite war of organic beings, which is going on in peaceful woods and smiling fields."[1] For Darwin the peaceful and pastoral façade of nature conceals a bloody and deadly chronicle of violence that, at least for him, made the whole idea of providence questionable. When I was writing my book, *God After Darwin*, I received a letter from a man in North Carolina, who introduced himself to me as an ordained Protestant minister who, late in life, had decided to look up close at the Darwinian picture of nature. He confessed that he had come away from that experience with the conviction that he could no longer be a clergyman. Not only did he feel obliged to give up the ministry, but he could no longer be a

Christian or a believer at all. So he now refers to himself as an atheist. In his letter, and later in a book that he also sent me, he went on at great length asking questions like this:

Could an Almighty God of love have designed, foreseen, planned, and created a system whose law is a ruthless struggle for existence in an overcrowded world? Could an omnipotent, omniscient, and omnibenevolent God have devised such a cold-blooded competition of beast with beast, beast with man, man with man, species with species, in which the clever, the cunning, and the cruel survive?

How could a loving God have planned a cruel system in which sensitive, living creatures must either eat other sensitive, living creatures or be eaten themselves, thereby causing untold suffering among these creatures? Would a benevolent God have created animals to devour others when he could have designed them all as vegetarians? What kind of deity would have designed the beaks which rip sensitive flesh? What God would intend every leaf, blade of grass, and drop of water to be a battle ground in which living organisms pursue, capture, kill, and eat one another? What God would design creatures to prey upon one another and, at the same time, instill into such creatures a capacity for intense pain and suffering?[2]

My correspondent here is raising the classic question of theodicy. Darwin, of course, is not the first to turn our attention to this issue, but for many educated people his evolutionary picture of life exacerbates the theodicy problem beyond the pale of any human speculation to respond adequately. Why, in any conceivably divine plan, did there have to take place all the epochs of life's struggle and suffering? In his autobiography, Darwin asks: "What advantage can there be in the suffering of millions of the lower animals throughout almost endless time?"[3] I suppose that the natural theologian William Paley would have remarked at how exquisitely the teeth of alligators are adapted or designed to crushing the flesh of other animals so as to be able to survive. And Asa Gray, a Harvard botanist, as well as a friend and defender of Darwin in the US, would have opined that Darwinism doesn't destroy the design argument for God's existence, but simply widens it. Darwin himself, however, didn't buy the idea: Why, he asked, would God design wasps that lay their eggs in caterpillars so that when the larvae hatch out they'll have fresh meat to live on? It is impossible, if you believe in a beneficent

God, to imagine that divine providence would directly plan such a crude instrument of creativity as evolution seems to be.

Look, for example, at the life cycle of the sheep liver fluke. Let me summarize Sir Charles Sherrington's description of it. There is a parasite, he says, that lives near our ponds. It produces larvae that swim into the water and penetrate snails living there. The little worms tend to eat the snail up from the inside, and, having been fed, they swim to the edge of the pond and encyst themselves on the vegetation there. Then a sheep or cow will eat the grass, ingesting the cyst in which the worms have encased themselves. The cyst will dissolve in the digestive juices of the sheep or cow's stomach. Then the worms will crawl out, making their way into the liver of the host where they will cause enormous discomfort. The worms reach maturity in the bile ducts and then are passed out into the pasture via the host animal's feces. Then they hatch out and go back into more snails. In such a fashion the cycle continues age after age.

What is going on here? To Sherrington. . . it is a story of securing existence to a worm at cost of lives superior to it in the scale of life as humanly reckoned. Life's prize is given to the aggressive and inferior of life, destructive of other lives at the expense of suffering in them, and, sad as it may seem to us, suffering in proportion as they are lives high in life's scale. The example taken is a fair sample of almost countless many.[4]

Why all this suffering? Darwin's answer was that suffering is simply an adaptive characteristic of beings endowed with sensitive nervous systems. If they don't suffer then they won't stand out of harm's way, and consequently they won't be able to survive and be reproductively successful. Darwin thought that one could explain suffering — this is his "theodicy" as it were — in purely naturalistic terms, namely, as adaptation. Today, scientists have gone beyond Darwin. Evolutionary systems theory understands suffering in more informational terms, interpreting pain as life's negative feedback mechanism. Negative feedback may be defined as information about the difference between an actual state and an ideal state, as in the thermostat in this room. Suffering then is information that a living organism is not in an ideally adaptive condition.

Another contemporary interpretation of suffering is that of Richard Dawkins and others influenced by sociobiology. From a gene's-eye perspective suffering, like sex and other characteristics, is something that the genes of organisms have invented so as to make their survival more probable. Genes somehow sense that they need to construct vehicles that are sensitive to pain. Otherwise, the vehicle will be destroyed and the genes will not gain entry into the next generation. So, from a purely gene-centered point of view, the reason for suffering is very clear and can be understood in a very naturalistic sort of way. Dawkins, one of the world's best-known evolutionists and a writer who comes close to identifying Darwinism with atheism, admits that Darwin's ". . . is not a recipe for happiness. So long as DNA is passed on, it does not matter who or what gets hurt in the process. It is better for the genes of Darwin's ichneumon wasp that the caterpillar should be alive, and therefore fresh, when it is eaten, no matter what the cost in suffering. Genes don't care about suffering, because they don't care about anything."[5]

According to Dawkins, Darwin's ideas provide the surest intellectual foundation atheism has ever had.[6] And the philosopher Daniel Dennett concurs. He argues that Dawkins's gene's-eye interpretation of evolution amounts to a definitive "scientific" refutation of theology. Dennett's work is an obvious challenge to anyone who embraces modern science but yet continues to embrace the doctrine of providence.[7] And Dawkins and Dennett are by no means alone. For example, William Provine, a Cornell professor of the history of science, and a personal acquaintance of mine, comes closer than Dawkins and Dennett to identifying Darwinian biology with atheism. He admits that before the "modern synthesis" of genetics and Darwinism, also known as neo-Darwinism, came along, theological interpretations of evolution were entirely plausible. But once we learned to understand the role of genes in the story of life, no room remained for divine influence. Now, Provine says, any biologists who think there is still room for divine action in nature must "check their brains at the church-house door."[8]

In his book *Climbing Mount Improbable* Dawkins goes on to say that Darwinism is sufficient to explain not only suffering, but also everything else about life. He asks his readers to imagine a mountain on one side of which there is a sheer, vertical drop-off to the plane below. On the other side there is a gentler slope upward. If life had only a biblical period of six to ten thousand years to move up the first side, progressing from the state of simplicity to that of complex organisms, then Dawkins would forgive us for appealing to the notion of divine providence. Without a miraculous boost the eye or brain could not have been created in such a short amount of time. But let us go around to the other side of the mountain where we'll encounter, more realistically, the appropriate terrain of Darwinian evolution. On the gradual slope the long trail of life meanders back and forth lazily over the course of roughly four billion years. If we stir the other two ingredients of Darwin's recipe, randomness and natural selection, in with the enormity of time that life has had available to it, the evolution of complexity out of simplicity is much more probable. It can be understood purely naturalistically, and so there is no need to appeal to divine providence. Therefore, as Dawkins claimed earlier in *The Blind Watchmaker*, it is now possible to be an intellectually fulfilled atheist. If you were not an atheist before Darwin, you are forgiven. But after Darwin, there is no longer any excuse.[9]

2) Many contemporary biologists agree with Dawkins, as do lot of philosophers. But one response to their extreme position is to say: "Not so fast. Let's look at the whole cosmic picture. Biologists tend to focus on only one segment of a much larger story. Let's back up and look at the whole cosmic story that sponsors biological evolution. Maybe we can discern the hand of divine providence in the initial fine-tuning that was discussed in the previous lecture. A very precise expansion rate, gravitational force and other cosmic constants and initial conditions may have been front-loaded by God into this story we call the cosmos."

All well and good. However, the question still remains as to why God would choose the Darwinian formula as the way to create diversity in life. By taking the distant cosmic perspective, haven't we still ignored the theological difficulties that arise from the biologist's awareness of the blindness and brutality of evolution? Yes, there is creativity and cooperation in evolution. But there is also an awful lot of waste, suffering and struggle. We still have to make sense of that.

My point is, a lot of sensitive people are not impressed by the initial cosmic design argument, especially if the initial cosmic design seems only to make room for what is too often a horrifying story of life. Because of the indifference of natural selection, George Williams, one of the chief representatives of contemporary evolutionary biology, refers to mother nature as "a wicked old witch."[10]

And, as we have already seen, Dawkins take no pains to avoid saying also that the evolutionary story is not a nice one, even if it produced us.

3) What Darwin has uncovered is enough to make many religious people turn their eyes away in complete denial. But there are others who are willing to swallow the bitter pill, with the proviso that humans should not try too hard to understand what God may be doing in evolution. Darwin is not wrong, but for all we poor mortals know, behind the accidents, struggle and striving of evolution there lies a hidden divine plan. Maybe we use terms like accident, contingency and absurdity because of our human ignorance of the deeper plan. Maybe, from a God's-eye perspective, as the poet Alexander Pope puts it, chance (or contingency) is "direction which thou canst not see" simply because you don't have a divine vantage point.

I suppose the thinking here goes something like this: We humans all have a very limited understanding of what constitutes good order and design. And so whenever anything takes place that doesn't fit into our own frame of intelligibility, we tend to refer to it as an accident, contingency or even an absurdity. But, maybe there's a wider vision of things, and within that vision what we consider to be irrational make very good sense.

4) I suppose also that almost any theological response to the question of providence after Darwin must possess at least a touch of the intellectual humility recommended by the fideist approach just described. We humans have to admit that we shall never gain an absolutely clear perspective on anything. Still, the question remains whether theology has to remain satisfied with mere silence on the meaning of evolution. After all, isn't theology "faith seeking understanding"? Here there is a great divide. Some would contend that we should cut short all inquiry with acts of blind faith, and not try to figure things out at all. But others insist that a bold faith must at least try to understand what's going on, especially in the story of life, even if we can never attain full comprehension. Moreover, it is not a mark of faith and trust that we would simply put to death our intellects. We should at least struggle to understand what's going on, in this case what the Darwinian recipe is all about.

One example of this bolder theological approach is to speculate that evolution is a kind of divine pedagogy. The thinking here is that if life never had to suffer or struggle, if it were never challenged, it would have remained forever at the level of listless triviality. It would never have gotten anywhere significant without having to struggle. Extending this to the human domain, how anemic of character would we be if we never had to face obstacles or challenges? Is it possible then that the world we live in, the one in which life unfolds according to Darwinian rules, is something like a soul school or, more broadly, a school for life. Without life's having to traverse the Darwinian terrain, could we or other forms of life have ever acquired the complexity that makes high degrees of experience, and eventually consciousness, possible?

There are a number of representatives of this perspective. A very sophisticated one is the philosopher of religion, John Hick. In his book *Evil and the God of Love* he attempts to make sense of life's suffering by saying that, at least in humans, it serves the cause of "soul-making."[11] The idea is an ancient one, and examples are sprinkled throughout the scriptures. You can find the idea that God practices tough love, disciplining those that God loves, even in the New Testament, especially in Hebrews 12, 5ff. And the idea has quite a venerable pedigree in subsequent Christian literature and spirituality.

I have found a very accessible version of this "soul-school" theodicy in a book by science writer Guy Murchie, *The Seven Mysteries of Life*. In this book Murchie says we have to admit that the Darwinian process is harsh. But it is also educational, and that is enough to redeem it. Think of the earth as a soul school in which the severe Darwinian recipe is essential to the development and enhancement of life. This is enough to make the process providential. Murchie asks you to imagine that you are the creator. Could you make a better world than this one? He is thinking of the world in which Darwinian processes shape the course of life. This, he says, is the most "educational" environment you could imagine. Earth, it is true, carries innumerable strange species: "creatures are not only walking, creeping and slithering all over the land, but burrowing under it, climbing the trees above it, swimming in the seas around it, flying through the air, even dwelling invisibly within each other, trying out . . . every imaginable mode of locomotion, of communication, of preying, eating, sheltering, and propagating their kind." This life-word, Murchie agrees, is also one that harbors "heartrending struggles with adversity," and for us humans "social uncertainty."

Nonetheless, the Darwinian environment "excels in educating the spirit." It is "far and away the top-ranking Soul School available."

Honestly now, if you were God, could you possibly dream up any more educational, contrastive, thrilling, beautiful, tantalizing world than Earth to develop spirit in? If you think you could, do you imagine you would be outdoing Earth if you designed a world free of germs, diseases, poisons, pain, malice, explosives and conflicts so its people could relax and enjoy it? Would you, in other words, try to make the world nice and safe — or would you let it be provocative, dangerous and exciting? In actual fact, if it ever came to that, I'm sure you would find it impossible to make a better world than God has already created.[12]

What are we to make of this interpretation? As is true of the previous approach, it does at least have the merit of not trying to edit out or cover up the harsher evolutionary facts. On the other hand, it raises some troubling theological questions. Why, for example, do all the other species have to go to school with us? And couldn't a lot less suffering be just as pedagogical as a large amount? This is what bothered Darwin. Why, he wondered, is suffering so excessive if God is good? And many other sensible people have trouble with the idea of pain as divine pedagogy. Maybe the "soul school" interpretation is part of a larger set of truths, but by itself it hardly seems satisfactory.

5) This was certainly the opinion of Teilhard de Chardin (for an introduction to whose views on evolution please see the previous lecture). Teilhard questioned the view that all the suffering in evolution could be understood simply in terms of either expiation or education. Instead he placed the solution to the problem of suffering within the biblical horizon of *expectation* of future redemption. Teilhard does not pretend to give a satisfying answer to the theodicy question. But he invites us to place the question of evolutionary suffering within the framework of an unfinished universe, and only then ask what the meaning of such suffering might be. What evolution implies, before anything else, is that the universe is still unfinished. Theologically speaking, the fact of evolution means that the universe has not yet been fully created. And because the universe is unfinished, it is now imperfect by definition. And if it is imperfect, then it is possible for it to have a dark aspect or shadow side to it. What we experience as suffering and evil somehow gains a foot-

hold in the very fact that the universe is unfinished and therefore imperfect.

From a Teilhardian perspective all the things that bother us, all the big questions that we ask in life, are a function of the fact that we live in an unfinished universe. Why does life struggle and suffer in the first place? Why do we have to walk by faith rather than by sight? Why does God remain hidden? Why is atheism possible? Why are our religions so imperfect?

All of this has something to do with the fact that the universe is not yet finished.

For Teilhard, therefore, there is no speculative answer to the question of suffering. But there can be a *response*. The response is to hope. Life is always, from start to finish, a kind of groping exploration. And at the human level, once we appear in evolution, the way in which the groping of evolution takes place is through the hoping of human beings for a new future up ahead, one in which evil and suffering will be conquered. That's the appropriate response to evil, not to be passive about it, but to do something about it, to make a world in which suffering becomes less and less.

But then the question becomes: Why would a good, providential God, a God who truly cares for us and for the world, make an unfinished universe in the first place? Teilhard's answer is that there is really no alternative, theologically speaking, to an unfinished initial creation. An originally perfect creation — an idea that seemed tenable before we became aware of the unfolding, unfinished character of the universe — is in any case theologically inconceivable. Why? Because if you try to imagine the Creator, in the beginning, making a perfectly finished, fully complete world, such a world would not be distinct from God. It would not be *other* than God. Keep in mind the principle of Teilhard's that I talked about in the previous lecture: True union differentiates. This principle means here that the actual union of God with the world requires — and I think this is the essential Christian intuition — that the world must be *differentiated* from God. God can unite in love only to what is other than God (or, in Trinitarian language, only to the otherness within God). So if the world were created perfectly in the beginning, then this world would be nothing more than an extension of God's own being, or an appendage of deity, rather than something distinct from God.

Not just Christianity but Islam and Judaism as well have always emphasized that God is not the world. They have persistently rejected pantheism, against the constant resistance of those who find monotheism too demanding. This means that the world must in some sense be radically other than God. And so, I would suggest that divine providence, by definition, desires to sustain the otherness of the world in the very process of caring or providing for it. Understanding this tension is important in any attempt to coordinate general divine providence with the waywardness of evolution. As far as the doctrine of creation is concerned, we may assume that an initially perfect world could not be truly *other* than God. For the world to be other than God it has to be given the opportunity to *become* itself. In other words, it has to be given permission to experiment with new possibilities of being. And this, evolution seems to be telling us, is what is happening.

An originally perfect world might be a world without suffering. But it would also be a world without a future because everything would have been fixed in place once and for all. It would also be a world without freedom, because every event, including human action, would be determined from the very start to be just what it is. There would be no indeterminacy, freedom, or even contingency— all essential if the world is to stay open to the newness of the future. And so an originally perfect world would be one without life, which requires that physical systems remain open to an indefinite array of new arrangements. Consequently there can really be no reasonable theological alternative to an unfinished universe. And so, at least in the Teilhardian view of things, the unfinished character of the universe is itself providential.[13]

6) Another religious vision of the cosmos that successfully accommodates the Darwinian recipe is that of Alfred North Whitehead and his followers.[14] I noted in the previous lecture that Whitehead views the universe as an aim toward beauty. But this aim is not always successful, and since God is persuasive rather than coercive, there is going to be room for meandering around and experimenting with various possibilities as the universe unfolds. There will also be room for struggle, suffering and tragedy.

The tragedy in life, such as the Darwinian picture brings to light, is something that Whitehead takes very seriously. But he proposes that tragedy can be conquered by beauty. There is no way one can prove this, but Whitehead can point to the way in which ancient Greek drama, for example, provided a kind of salvific framework for the experience of tragedy and suffering in the lives of struggling people. Many of us have found that the experience of being carried away by great beauty renews our hope and allows us to anticipate the culmination of the whole cosmos in a divine vision that will transform contrasts and contradictions into a final Perfection of beauty.

Accordingly, Whitehead thinks of God's providential will not as preventing suffering, but at least as providing an aesthetic framework for the resolution of the absurdity of all suffering. The suffering of the world contributes to what Whitehead calls the "wider vision" of things that occurs in God's own experience. There is suffering, but there is also redemption. The point I'm trying to make here is that process thought has very little difficulty accommodating the evolutionary biological perspective. In contemporary theological discussions of evolution, process thought has to be taken seriously, though not uncritically.

7) However, I have not yet spoken about evolution and providence in a strictly theological way. And so it is as a theologian that I would now like to approach the topic of this lecture. Theologians, unlike philosophers and scientists, are obliged to speak about the world, including the natural world, from the perspective of the faith community or tradition to which they belong. Theologians don't speak from nowhere, or from some universally objective point of view, as though they could look down on things from above. Rather, they speak about the world from within the framework of the concepts, sensibilities, ideas, symbols, stories and doctrines that are given in their tradition. For me it is from the Christian and specifically Catholic tradition that I attempt to relate evolution to theology.

Michael Ruse, an agnostic and self-avowed Darwinian materialist, has written a thoughtful book entitled *Can a Darwinian Be a Christian?* One way for a theologian to approach the question of evolution, on the other hand, is to ask whether a Christian can be a Darwinian? This question is still very much on the minds of a lot of Christians today, even as it was in Darwin's own time. Maybe you have resolved the issue in your own mind, but many Christians that

I meet and read about have not done so. Here then are some of my own thoughts on this very divisive issue.

Can a Christian be a Darwinian? Not if Darwinism means materialism, as it does even for many of our best evolutionists. Materialism is the philosophical belief or worldview that takes matter—lifeless and mindless matter — to be the most fundamental reality, the ultimate ground from which everything else springs, including life and mind. However, I am convinced that materialism is not essential to evolution. Teilhard and Whitehead, as I have just pointed out, are examples of great thinkers who consider materialist philosophy an obstacle to the understanding of what is really going on in evolution. Unfortunately Phillip Johnson and others in the Intelligent Design community, as well as many among creationists, agree with scientists like Dawkins who identify evolutionary science with materialist philosophy. Likewise, Stephen Jay Gould never tired of saying that the reason that people can't accept evolution is not that it is a difficult notion conceptually. In fact the Darwinian recipe is easy to understand. The reason people can't accept it, Gould complained, is that it brings along with it a "philosophical message" that is impalatable to most people. Darwin's message, he says, is that there is no direction to life—he detested Teilhard's idea that there is an overall direction to life. Darwin's theory implies for Gould that there is no purpose in the universe and that matter is all there is.[15] For Gould the philosophy of materialism is stitched seamlessly into evolutionary science itself. Of course, materialism is an inherently atheistic belief-system, so when some notable Darwinians themselves write that evolution is inseparable from materialism, then it would seem to those who take this association seriously that there is no way in which Christianity can accommodate evolution.

But what I have been struggling to do for many years — and what I think others in the theological community are doing also — is to distinguish the information that science gathers in the fossil record, radiometric dating, biogeographical distribution, comparative anatomy, genetics and so on, from the arbitrary materialist overlay that some evolutionists superimpose on their accounts of the unfolding of life. It is possible, I believe, to take the painfully garnered scientific data pertaining to evolution and contextualize it within a theological framework. This framework is opposed to materialism but not to the *science* of evolution. In any case, I don't think it is necessary to identify evolutionary science or the information that feeds into evolutionary science, with materialist philosophy.

If what I have just said is plausible, then I would go on to argue that Christians can accept a providential God, not in spite of, but *because* of evolution's recipe. The threefold recipe that I have been talking about from the beginning — contingency, lawful constraints such as natural selection, and lots and lots of time — can be accommodated quite easily by a providential understanding. From a theological point of view, remember that if we accept the Christian perspective on things — and I'm not assuming that everybody will follow me here—we are instructed not to think about God without thinking first of all about the man Jesus. Christians believe that it is in this man, in his life, that the image of God is made manifest in all of its fullness. And this means that when we reflect on evolution we should not start with the idea of a divine designer or engineer and then try to reconcile that idea with evolution. Instead let us start from the specifically Christian understanding of God that we are given by our faith tradition. And this is an understanding that takes shape in terms of the image of God as revealed in the person, deeds, life, death and resurrection of Jesus the Christ.

Now there are many ways in which one can unfold what this image implies. Here I shall simplify the task and focus on three aspects of the God-image as manifest in the biblical portraits of Jesus. There are 1) the fact of Jesus' humility as disclosed in his obedience unto death, 2) his self-giving love, and 3) his power to open up the future to those who were at dead ends in their lives. This latter feature is Jesus' implementation of the essential biblical theme of promise, and it is why it was so easy for the early Christians to configure the New Testament in continuity with the Hebrew scriptures in which the theme of divine promise is central. So when theology asks whether evolution is compatible with divine providence, it should not think of divine providence as in any way separate from these three aspects: 1) the humility of God that is revealed to us in the image of Christ; 2) the self-giving character of God made manifest in Jesus' giving himself up to the point of death; and 3) the identity of God as one who makes promises, as made visible in the way Jesus opens up the future to those who are lost, rejected, sick and even dead. Let us now take each of these three attributes and look at evolution in its light.

1) Evolution and the humility of God. Humility is not a concept that everyone associates immediately with God. As Whitehead himself observes, when Christianity came into the West it was the image of Caesar rather than that of the humble man of Nazareth that came to dominate our imaging of God. But a true revolution of religion and theology is implied in the Christian theme of the humility of God. The main classic source for this revolution is Chapter 2 of St. Paul's letter to the Philippians. In this chapter Paul quotes an early Christian hymn that pictures Jesus as being in the form of God. But not clinging to that status, he is portrayed as emptying himself, as undergoing a *kenosis* (the Greek word for emptying), and taking on the form of a slave. We don't have to ground the notion of divine humility simply in one Scriptural passage since the Gospels all implicitly make the same point. The whole story of God's anointed one being brought to crucifixion depicts the *kenosis* or self-emptying of the Christ. Subsequent reflection by theology on Philippians 2 and the Gospels, however, has often concluded that what is really being emptied out in the *kenosis* of Jesus is the being of God whose essence according to Christian doctrine and creeds is conjoined to that of Christ. The Gospels and early Christian writings are telling the story, in other words, of the descent of God.

And so, in the light of this strange new kenotic view of deity, what should the world look like?[16] What kind of a world can we "predict," to use a scientific term, on the basis of the "hypothesis" of a vulnerable, self-emptying God? Jürgen Moltmann, a well-regarded Protestant theologian, has argued that in the light of God's *kenosis* even the creation of the world should be looked upon as the effect of the divine self-humbling. Referring to Jewish Cabbalistic thought as well as to the theme of the crucified God, Moltmann concludes that it is only by God's contracting, shrinking or "withdrawing" the divine omnipresence and omnipotence, that a space is opened up for something other than God to come into being.[17] It is God's humility that makes possible the existence of the world in the first place, and that allows the world to remain distinct from God. We have here the primordial instance of Teilhard's notion that true union differentiates. God wants the world to be different from God, to be distinct from God. It is only such a distinct world that can actually take up a true union, an intense, intimate dialogical *communion* with God.

So the first act of creation is an act of "othering," of letting something other than God come into being. And making room for the other, as we know from our own experience, requires a self-withdrawal, in a sense. In the case of God such a self-withdrawal is not an abdication of divine providence, but paradoxically the deepest kind of care for the wellbeing of the other, in this case the universe as such. So once again, for Moltmann, as for Teilhard, an instantaneously perfect creation would be theologically inconceivable. The notion of an initially perfect creation would be inconsistent with the idea of God's allowing something other than God to come into existence. And if there is room for a creation that is truly other than God, then maybe the world would be given ample scope by God for experimenting with many possibilities of being. And perhaps life would be allowed and even encouraged to wander about searching for adaptive formats, precisely in the way that evolutionary science depicts. And it would also be consistent with such a world that it would take lots and lots of time to come up with living and thinking beings.

So here God's providence is expressed in an everlasting concern that the creation be granted every opportunity to become *other* than God. This does not mean that the world is separate or cut off from God. Remember, true union differentiates! It is the world's difference from God that makes true (dialogical) union with God possible, and vice-versa. Wolfhart Pannenberg, another Protestant theologian whom I should mention here, has also said that what God wills is the independence of creation. And so, the whole evolutionary world that science has uncovered is one that Pannenberg as well as Moltmann and many others now think makes eminently good sense theologically: God cares for the world so much that God wants the world to be other than God, and hence to *become* itself, a process that apparently takes an enormous amount of time.

This is a much deeper form of care than can be found in the more manipulative deities that we often wish for. And, at the same time, this kenotic view of God does not envisage God as aloof or holding back, in deistic detachment from the world. Rather God participates in the cross of the Christ, and by implication in all the world's struggle and suffering. Indeed there is no evolutionary struggle and suffering that occurs outside of the divine compassion itself.

2) Let's look now at the second idea about God that we associate with the Gospel portraits of Jesus. It is one that overlaps, of course, with the theme of divine humility. I am referring here to the idea of God as absolute self-giving love. Karl Rahner can be our guide here. Rahner was a Jesuit priest and arguably the most important Roman Catholic theologian of the twentieth century. He claimed that Christianity is not terribly complicated as a religion, when you get down underneath it all. Christianity has two foundational beliefs. First, it shares with other religions the belief that there is a great Mystery, ineffable and incomprehensible, that grounds and sustains the universe, a Mystery that we call God. And secondly Christianity believes, on the basis of its own revelatory sources, that this ultimate, infinite, inexpressible, God seeks to give the divine infinity away unreservedly to the creation, to the finite world. This is the meaning of the Christ-event, namely, that the infinite God has given the divine self away completely to the world. And this means in turn that what we call "revelation" is not first and foremost a set of propositions or doctrines, but God's *self*-communication. It is the being of God that is revealed as self-giving love.[18]

If this is so, then, by anybody's mathematics that which is infinite cannot be received fully in any one instant. So the finite world, if you want to use a Darwinian word here, has to "adapt" to the Infinite. Therefore, it cannot stand still, but has to undergo a process of expanding its being in the presence of the self-giving Infinite. That is, it is invited to keep going beyond itself. The outward appearance of that process of self-transcendence is what we refer to as evolution. So Christianity, if we think about it in depth, already "predicts" an evolutionary world — not chronologically but systematically speaking. Christianity already suggests from within its own principles of faith that the finite universe, including life, simply cannot stand still, but will always remain restless until it is taken up into the infinite. This is just an extension to the cosmos of Augustine's principle that our hearts are restless until they rest in God. The cosmos is restless until it is taken fully and finally into the mystery of the divine. Once again, then, evolution occurs not in spite of but because of the providence of God.

3) Finally, from a Christian theological point of view, we should never disassociate the theme of providence, as unfortunately we often do anyway, from the biblical theme of promise. Every teach-

ing of Christianity, as Moltmann says, has to be seen in light of the theme of promise. Promise is the fundamental theme, and so Christianity is essentially about the future.[19] The biblical God is one who calls Abraham into a new future, and so in Biblical faith, providence must be tied always to the coming of the future. The word of God that hovers over creation in the beginning is the same word of promise that Israel associated with God's call to Abraham. God's word, in other words, is one that always opens up the future, and that is ultimately why we have an evolving universe. Instead of seeing the universe as seeded with strict "design," my preference theologically is to view the world as seeded with promise. It is not so much that design is front-loaded into the universe as that the universe is seeded with promise from the very beginning.

The advantage of thinking in terms of promise rather than design is that promise is consistent with present ambiguity and the unfinished character of the universe. If you keep emphasizing that God is a designer, and then look around and open your eyes, you will notice that the world is not perfectly designed at all. Very few if any evolutionary adaptations, for example, can be said to be perfect. Often the world seems very messy. But if the universe is rooted in promise and still has a future, this would be consistent with present imperfection and ambiguity. On this score, I think that Intelligent Design advocates paint themselves into a corner when they keep emphasizing design. To do so simply exacerbates the theodicy problem: if God is the designer, then why is there so much suffering and so much evil? If God can design irreducible complexity at the heart of cells, why doesn't God design life in such a way as not to struggle and suffer? I think that the theological problem here is that intelligent design is entirely too stiff and too lifeless a term to represent the way in which a promising God interacts with an unfinished universe. On the other hand, the theme of promise gives us hope that eventually, eschatologically speaking, all of life's suffering will be redeemed by and in God. Let's remember also that the word providence comes from the Latin *pro-video* which means "to look forward" into the future. Maybe it would be appropriate for us to think of God's *vision* or maybe even God's *dream* for the universe, instead of God's design for the universe, as the ultimate context of evolution.

It would seem to me, therefore, that Darwin's three-part recipe would fit quite nicely into the theological theme of nature as promise. First of all, the fact of contingency could be interpreted not as absurdity, which is how Jacques Monod, Stephen Jay Gould and others have interpreted contingency, but as a necessary condition for nature's being open to a new future. Just think of the alternative: a universe devoid of contingency would be so frozen, stiff and dead that it could not have anything like an opening to the future.

Then there are the laws of nature, such as natural selection, regularities that are so unbending that the universe appears impersonal at heart. But you could argue that the lawful predictability in nature is completely consonant with the providential theme of divine fidelity. Try to imagine a world without lawful consistency to it, without some sort of habituality that we can depend upon. Such a world at every moment could just dissolve into the jelly of complete disarray. It would not possess the backbone that it needs in order to have continuity through time, a consistency that is indispensable to its having a future as well. So I think it is possible to correlate the element of necessity, along with the element of contingency in evolution, with the theme of divine promise.

And finally, what bothers a lot of people about evolution is that if God really cared about life, why didn't life come about at the beginning of the universe, rather than only four billion years ago? If God really cared about life, why would it take so much time to appear? Why all the "fooling around" that evolution puts up with? The fact of deep time and the gradualism of evolution are deeply offensive to some Christians. For them perhaps the most repellant feature of evolution is that so many millions of years seem to have been "wasted" before humans came onto the scene.

I don't know how you deal with this matter, but I've found that the theme of "divine patience" is a nice way of formulating divine care. Perhaps patience and waiting can be the deepest and most compassionate ways of expressing care — as, for example, in our own relationship to our children. Listen to these words of Moltmann. God, he says, ". . . acts in the history of nature and human beings through a patient and silent presence, giving creatures space to unfold, time to develop, and power for their own movement." The power to let the other be, in other words, is manifested in letting the other have its own movement. And God is willing to wait, to allow the world ample time to become itself. "Waiting," Moltmann continues, "keeps an open space for the other." Sometimes, he argues, waiting is the deepest expression of care. And so, God's waiting for the world to unfold by way of evolution may also be a profound expression of God's providence.[20]

Notes

[1] Cited in Richard Dawkins, *A Devil's Chaplain: Selected Essays* (London: Orion Books, 2004), 10.

[2] A. J. Mattill, Jr., *The Seven Mighty Blows to Traditional Beliefs*, 2nd Edition (Gordo, Alabama: The Flatwoods Press, 1995), 32.

[3] Nora Barlow, editor, *The Autobiography of Charles Darwin* (New York: Harcourt, 1958), 88-89.

[4] Charles Sherrington, *Man on His Nature* (Cambridge: Cambridge University Press, 1951), 266.

[5] Richard Dawkins, *River Out of Eden*, (New York: Basic Books, 1995), 131.

[6] Richard Dawkins, *The Blind Watchmaker*, (New York: W. W. Norton & Co., 1986) 6.

[7] Daniel C. Dennett, *Darwin's Dangerous Idea: Evolution and the Meaning of Life* (New York: Simon & Schuster, 1995).

[8] William Provine, "Evolution and the Foundation of Ethics," in Steven L. Goldman, ed., *Science, Technology and Social Progress* (Bethlehem, Pa.: Lehigh University Press, 1989), 261.

[9] Richard Dawkins, *Climbing Mount Improbable* (New York: W. W. Norton & Co., 1996).

[10] Williams, George C., "Mother Nature Is a Wicked Old Witch!" in Matthew H. Nitecki and Doris V. Nitecki, eds., *Evolutionary Ethics* (Albany, NY: State University of New York Press, 1995), 217-231.

[11] See John Hick, *Evil and the God of Love* (Norfolk, England: The Fontana Library, 1968), 333-38.

[12] Guy Murchie, *The Seven Mysteries of Life: An Exploration in Science and Philosophy* (Boston: Houghton Mifflin, 1978), 621-22.

[13] These thoughts are based on my reading of many works of Teilhard, but especially the essays in Pierre Teilhard de Chardin, *Christianity and Evolution*, trans. René Hague (New York: Harcourt Brace & Co., 1969).

[14] For the following see especially Whitehead's *Adventures of Ideas*.

[15] Stephen Jay Gould, *Ever Since Darwin* (New York: W. W. Norton, 1977), 12-13.

[16] Incidentally, sometimes I have been accused, especially by scientific skeptics, of twisting and accommodating the Christian message so that it fits the Darwinian picture of life. But I am able to point out that my theology is not so marginal after all. Even as conservative an interpreter of Christianity as John Paul II, in his encyclical *Fides et Ratio* states that the fundamental concern of Christian theology is to explore the significance of the *kenosis*, that is, the self-emptying of God.

[17] Jürgen Moltmann, *God in Creation*, trans. by Margaret Kohl (San Francisco: Harper & Row, 1985), 88.

[18] Karl Rahner, *Foundations of Christian Faith: An Introduction to the Idea of Christianity*,

trans. by William V. Dych (New York : Seabury Press 1978).

[19] Jürgen Moltmann, *Theology of Hope*, trans. by James Leitch (New York: Harper and Row, 1967), 16.

[20] Jürgen Moltmann, "God's Kenosis in the Creation and Consummation of the World," John Polkinghorne, editor, *The Work of Love: Creation as Kenosis* (Grand Rapids, Michigan: Eerdman's Publishing Company, 2001), 149.

Lecture 3: On the Origin of Life

A question on the mind of many scientists and philosophers today is how to account for the origin of life. The question cannot be a matter of indifference to those of us who are interested in the relationship between theology and science. But where shall we locate theological explanation in relation to scientific accounts of life?

In the intellectual world today there is a powerful temptation to settle for purely naturalistic explanations of everything, and so I must begin by talking about *naturalism*. What I mean by naturalism is the belief that the world available to scientific inquiry is all there is. Nature, in this definition, includes humans and all our own creations. Naturalism would mean, then, that there is no room for the existence of any trans-empirical reality. The world is utterly godless, and theology a pointless discipline.

I suppose that almost anybody who has ever been impressed by the robust explanatory power of science may have wondered, at one time or another, whether there is a need for theology or any kinds of explanations other than those that science gives us. A lot of smart people would say absolutely not. Naturalism is quite enough for many in the scientific and philosophical worlds today. There are, of course, different ways of understanding naturalism — such varieties as religious naturalism, soft naturalism, hard naturalism and so forth. But I intend to use the term "naturalism" the way most philosophers, scientists and theologians use it, namely, to designate the belief that nature, as it is available to common experience and scientific method, is literally *all* there is.

The fundamental tenets of naturalism are these: To begin with, only the world of nature is real. But, since nature is all there is, nature must be self-originating. There is nothing outside of nature that could cause it to exist. And since there is nothing beyond it, nature has no goal that it could be striving toward, nothing in the order of teleology as Whitehead and Teilhard have proposed (see the previous two lectures). And, therefore, all causes must be natural causes. Consequently, there is no room for the miraculous. Every natural event is itself the product of other natural events. And finally, according to naturalists, there is no life beyond death. Nature is *really* all there is.[1]

Until not too long ago, naturalistic explanations seemed to be inadequate, even in the sciences. This was partly because vitalistic assumptions were widely accepted. "Vitalism," from the Latin word *vita* (life), is a philosophy that argues that in order for life to exist at all a nonmaterial force must intervene in nature and elevate lifeless matter to the status of life. Henri Bergson, the famous French vitalist philosopher, called this supra-material cause an *elan vital*, a "vital force" similar in many ways to what theists call God. According to vitalists, since there is something mysteriously supernatural about life, science can say very little about it. Until very recently, human life, ethics and religion were also off-limits to naturalistic explanation. Scientists did not dare to stray into any areas that were thought of as bordering on the spiritual. As we shall see in a moment, things are quite different today.

Another reason why there was so much resistance to naturalism is that the "perennial philosophy" shaped the consciousness of most people, including intellectuals in both West and East, until recently. By the "perennial philosophy" I mean the core teachings of the great philosophical and religious traditions of the world. Foremost among these common teachings is the belief that there is an ultimate reality, a transcendent source and goal of the world's being, hidden from empirical awareness. In the West we call it God, but different religions and worldviews would name it differently. A second persistent belief is that reality is structured hierarchically. Here we may follow E. F. Schumacher's book *A Guide for the Perplexed*, a handy compendium of the traditional perennial philosophy. If matter can be represented by the letter m, Schumacher writes, then plant life can be coded as $m+x$, where x stands for the elusive quality that plant life adds to the purely material level of reality. Animal forms of life, which bear the beginnings of consciousness, can be designated as $m+x+y$. And humans, who are not only conscious, but also conscious of being conscious, are portrayed as $m+x+y+z$. The point I want to emphasize here is that until very recently the emergence of x, y, and z in the hierarchy seemed to require a special divine principle to bring them about and sustain them in existence. Naturalism was inconceivable.[2]

A third assumption of the perennial philosophy was that the more real something is, the more elusive it is from the perspective of any lower level. Accordingly, life cannot be explained in terms of sciences such as physics and chemistry that deal with the level of matter. Even today most people, at least in the world of common sense and social existence, tend to follow the perennial philosophy's hierarchical view of nature. So it is a matter of great interest that naturalism — with its attendant reductionism — has become so dominant in the intellectual world today.

How did the dramatic transition from the perennial philosophy to the essentially lifeless world of contemporary scientific naturalism take place? There are different ways of telling the story, but a compelling one is that of the late Jewish philosopher Hans Jonas.[3] Jonas notes that human societies, up until about the time of Renaissance, were for the most part *panvitalistic*. That is, they thought that *all* of reality was somehow alive. Picture yourself in any pre-scientific tribal setting. You would experience the sky, the sun, the stars, the weather, rivers, rocks, trees, animals, everything, as pulsing with life. To the panvitalist life is the pervasive reality. But if life is the fundamental reality, then what is death? How can death be real? Suppose an animal or a person in your tribe dies, and the dead body is lying there in front of you. How can you make sense of such a strange phenomenon? The lifeless corpse simply does not fit into your panvitalistic world view. How can you understand something to be truly dead if everything *real* is alive?

That was a major problem for our ancestors. For them life was the norm, and death the unintelligible exception. Death therefore was considered unreal, an illusion. And so, in order to save the panvitalistic hypothesis, our ancestors came up with the idea of the *soul* as a permanent animating principle in organisms, a subjective center that still lives on even when there is the appearance of death. The essential core of living beings, animals as well as humans, survives. It may come back at times to haunt or to console, but it is more real than death.

This notion of the soul, of course, has been extremely comforting for millions upon millions of people throughout the ages. But by the time the modern period arrived, a pronounced soul-body dualism had taken hold, and it prepared the way for the infamous mind-matter dualism of Descartes, where mind or soul got expelled completely from the world of matter. After Descartes a sharp split arose between mind and matter, and this led logically to the assumption that the material world was fundamentally mindless—and, of course, also lifeless. The idea of an essentially lifeless and mindless realm of matter then served as the philosophical foundation of modern science and most naturalistic philosophies. Life and mind, accordingly, seem to have only the status of epiphenomena. They are held to be derivatives of something considered to be more real than they are, namely, matter. The *real* world is lifeless and mindless material stuff.

The theologian Paul Tillich aptly refers to this modern naturalistic view as an "ontology of death," meaning that what has the status of true being is deadness, not aliveness.[4] You can see then how the panvitalist problematic has been completely inverted. For our ancestors, life was the norm, and death the unintelligible exception that needed to be explained. Today, at least in much of the intellectual world, death is the norm, and it is life that begs for an explanation. Scientific research programs all over the world still operate on the background assumption that the universe is essentially dead, and they are trying to figure out how such an amazing thing as life could appear out of an inherently dead cosmos.

As Jonas puts it:

. . . from the physical sciences there spread over the conception of all existence an ontology whose model entity is pure matter, stripped of all features of life. What at the animistic

stage was not even discovered has in the meantime conquered the vision of reality, entirely ousting its counterpart.
The tremendously enlarged universe of modern cosmology
is conceived as a field of inanimate masses and forces which
operate according to the laws of inertia and of quantitative
distribution in space. This denuded substratum of all reality
could only be arrived at through a progressive expurgation
of vital features from the physical record and through strict
abstention from projecting into its image our own felt aliveness.[5]

And so, for modern scientific consciousness, "it is the existence
of life within a mechanical universe which now calls for an explanation, and explanation has to be in terms of the lifeless."[6] The explanation of the living in terms of what is dead continues to be the
methodological dream of much scientific research. Since life is said
to be composed of dead matter, the truly explanatory sciences must
therefore be chemistry and physics. The traditional lines of distinction that located humans, animals, plants and minerals on separate
ontological levels have disappeared, and lifeless "matter" has become dominantly explanatory in scientific attempts to understand
life and the universe. Some scientists and philosophers have recently
begun to question the cruder materialist reductionism dominant in
earlier attempts to account scientifically for life, but the philosophical foundation of most contemporary biology and neuroscience is
still predominantly an "ontology of death."

Obviously, we ourselves feel alive, but modern thought has told
us not to project our mentality and our own desire for warmth and
meaning onto the objectively lifeless and mindless world "out there."
A classic expression of this prohibition is the French biochemist
Jacques Monod's book Chance and Necessity, a work that appeared
in the late 1960s and became a bestseller.[7] It still stands today as a
monument to the Cartesian expurgation of life and mind from the
physical record. Jonas, however, would see the book as a vivid il-
lustration of the fact that for scientific thought in our time "the lifeless has become the knowable par excellence and is for that reason
also considered the true and only foundation of reality." Lifeless-
ness has come to be understood as "the 'natural' as well as the original state of things."[8] You may recall here the 30 volumes representing the 14 billion year old universe that I pictured in the first lecture:

the first twenty-two volumes consist of essentially lifeless stuff. Such a portrayal appears to support the view that dead matter is the mother of all things.

And so, a sense of the pervasive deadness and mindlessness of the universe undergirds the new methodological ideal, one unknown to most pre-scientific ways of looking at things. Today you can read in Francis Crick's book *Of Molecules and Men*, for example, that "the ultimate aim of the modern movement in biology is to explain all of life in terms of physics and chemistry."[9] Notice what an inversion of the perennial philosophy this is. All you need to focus on is the bottom level of the traditional hierarchy. If you understand that level well enough, then the whole ladder of being above matter can be explained in terms of the lowest rung. Crick's associate James Watson adds that "life will be completely understood in terms of the coordinated interactions of large and small molecules."[10] And philosopher Daniel Dennett, in speaking of the reducibility of mind, states that:

> ... there is only one sort of stuff, namely matter — the physical stuff of physics, chemistry, and physiology — and the mind is somehow nothing but a physical phenomenon. In short, the mind is the brain. According to the materialists we can (in principle!) account for every mental phenomenon using the same physical principles, laws and raw materials that suffice to explain radioactivity, continental drift, photosynthesis, reproduction, nutrition and growth.[11]

Finally, Owen Flanagan, a widely respected American philosopher, states in his book *The Problem of the Soul* (2003) that the whole purpose of philosophy is to make the world safe for the kind of materialist and reductionistic naturalism that Dennett espouses.[12] In fact, there are numerous philosophers today who agree with Flanagan that their discipline, far removed as it is from the "perennial" philosophy, should be promoting the idea that purely naturalistic explanations can account for everything.

Room for Theology?

So, in view of the intellectual respectability that naturalism claims today, can we find a place anywhere for theological explanation, and, if so, how? Traditionally, scholars made a distinction between primary and secondary causes: God was thought of as the ultimate or primary explanation of everything without having to be located somewhere among secondary or natural causes. However, I believe the science and religion conversation requires a slightly simpler approach today. So what I would propose is that we develop a taste for what I shall call "layered explanation." By layered explanation I mean that most things in our experience require a plurality of levels of explanation. Naturalism, on the other hand, is inclined toward explanatory monism, the belief that there is need for only one level of explanation, ideally the simplest. And it is natural science, according to naturalism, that has sole ownership of that level. The point is that there is no place for theological explanation.

Layered explanation, however, allows room for both theological and scientific understanding, in such a way that there can be no conflict or competition between them. But what would be a good example of layered explanation? I came across one somewhere in the voluminous writings of John Polkinghorne, but I shall modify it here considerably. Imagine that you have a pot of water boiling on your stove. A friend comes by and asks you why the pot is boiling. You can answer your friend's question by saying that it's boiling because the molecules of H_2O are moving around very excitedly and the content of the pot is making a transition from the liquid to the gaseous state. This is a very good explanation, and we should push it as far as possible. Still, this first layer of explanation does not disallow others. You may also respond to your friend's question by saying that the pot is boiling because you turned the gas on. This too is a good explanation, but it does not rule out still others. You might give a third explanation: the pot is boiling because you want to make tea. The point is, a full account of why the pot is boiling requires more than one layer. And again, each of the three layers of explanation may be pushed as far as it can possibly go without having to compete with the others. This is because each explanation, as I see it, is an abstraction from the totality of causal ingredients that enter into making the pot boil. Each layer is only one way of looking at something which, in order to explain it fully, requires that we take into account a rich plurality of factors.

Analogously, in conversations between scientists and theologians, we may regard both theological and scientific explanations as abstractions from the totality of causal elements that rich explanation needs to take into account. If we do so, there need be no competition between them. It would not make sense to say that the pot is boiling because of molecular motion *rather than* because I want a cup of tea. And you don't say it's boiling because I want tea *rather than* because somebody turned the gas on. Likewise, you don't have to say that life came about on earth because of chemical events *rather than* because God willed life to appear. And it is not logically necessary to agree with the naturalist that life came about because of certain chemical and physical occurrences *rather than* because of divine creativity.

In layered explanation the distinct accounts cannot be mapped onto each other. For example, you are not going to find "I want tea" inscribed in the steam that's coming from the pot of boiling water on your stove, even though your wanting tea is the "ultimate" explanation of the water's boiling. Completely different levels are involved here, and they need to be kept separate in our minds. In addition, the deepest explanations are always going to be the dimmest, or least clear, in terms of physical and mathematical representation. The elusiveness of deep explanation, of course, is annoying to the naturalist, who wants everything to be laid out with the same degree of clarity that we have come to expect from science. The modern naturalistic assumption has been that only clear and distinct ideas are fundamentally explanatory. But Alfred North Whitehead points out that this is a mistake: the things that are most clear and distinct are not at all the most fundamental. It is a logical mistake to think of them as fundamental since they are abstractions that have left out most of the causal factors in order to bring into focus a few quantifiable elements.[13]

Naturalism's aversion to deep explanation is consistent with its explanatory monism. The ancients, on the other hand, were quite comfortable with layered explanations. For example, in Plato's dialogue *Phaedo*, Socrates and his friends are conversing in his prison cell. The question comes up as to why Socrates is sitting there in jail. He answers: it is because "my body is composed of bones and sinews, and the bones are rigid and separated at the joints, but the sinews are capable of contraction and relaxation and form an envelope for the bones with the help of the flesh and the skin, the latter holding them all together; and since the bones move freely in their joints the sinews by relaxing and contracting enable me somehow to bend my limbs; and that is the cause of my sitting here in a bent position."[14]

This, of course, is a good explanation, but there can be other levels. What Socrates is trying to get across is the need for layered explanation. So he goes on to say that the deeper reason he's sitting there in prison is that the Athenians had condemned him for corrupting the youth of the city, and that he considered it "right and honorable" to accept their penalty. But even this response does not give the deepest reason for his sitting there: Socrates is sitting there because a transcendent Goodness—God, in other words—had grasped hold of him, and Socrates had surrendered his life to the calling of an eternal Goodness. This is the really important reason why he had been led to accept the Athenians' judgment and why he is sitting there in prison. Plato and Socrates were clearly comfortable with explanatory pluralism, whereas today's scientific naturalists are not.

So, with these examples in mind, let me return to the question of how theological explanation works. Here is my suggestion. I know it is not going to be satisfying to the naturalists, who want clear and distinct ideas. There is always going to be something fuzzy about theology—because it seeks a fundamental kind of explanation—and theology must neither apologize for that fact nor emulate the mathematical transparency of natural science. The language of theology is that of analogy. But here's how I suggest we think of theological explanation: divine influence stands in relation to the natural world, including such events as the origin of life, analogously to the way in which "I want tea" stands in relation to the molecular movement in the boiling pot of water. Or, to use my other example, divine action in nature works analogously to the way in which the attractive power of the Good influences the position of Socrates' bones and sinews.

My point is that even the most meticulous examination of the molecular movement in the pot of water is not going to reveal, at that level of explanation, the "I want tea" that hovers causally over the whole situation of the pot boiling. Nevertheless, the fact that I want tea is still the ultimate explanation of the water's boiling. Likewise, even the most thorough examination of Socrates' bones and sinews is not going to reveal, at that level of analysis, the power of the Good that explains ultimately why he's sitting there in his cell in prison. But to Socrates it is the hidden, though compelling, realm of divine goodness that most fundamentally accounts for his sitting in a prison cell. So the lesson I draw from these analogies is that even the most detailed scientific examination of nature, especially the sequence of physical events that led up to the emergence of the first living cell, is not going to reveal—and we should not expect it to do so—the ultimate reason why life came about in the universe at all. Nevertheless, it is in principle possible that such an ultimate explanation exists.

Let us look at some other examples of explanatory pluralism, just to reinforce the habit of mind it requires. Let's suppose, even at this hour of the day, that my brain is up here thinking as I speak to you. How are we to explain this fact? One very good explanation is that my neurons are firing, my synapses are connecting, my lobes are being activated — all the fascinating things that we are learning about in brain science. Again, this is a reasonable and essential explanation, and I would encourage neuroscientists to push it as far as they possibly can. But I can also answer the question "why am I thinking?" by saying that it is because of *my desire to understand* what is going on in the world. Now, it is true of course that the naturalist, especially the eliminative materialist or the hard reductionist, will try to map this second explanation completely onto the first. The dream of providing such a simplification is what gets materialist neuroscientists up in the morning. But this particular dream can never be fulfilled. This is "the hard problem" in cognitive science, as David Chalmers has called it.[15] There is no coherent way of mapping the first-person perspective that I take in my second explanation onto the third-person perspective that I use in the first. If one can accept the possibility of layered explanation, however, there should be no problem: both explanations are essential.

And now, to go even deeper, if you really want to understand why I am up here thinking, at some level the answer has to be: *because reality is intelligible*. If reality were not intelligible, my mind would not be working at all. Allow me then to use another analogy here. Just as the existence of light or photons has to be taken into account, at some level, when we explain why there are eyes, that is, why camera-like eyes have evolved independently some forty or more times, so likewise a necessary environment for the emergence of mind in evolution is that the universe be intelligible. As to why the universe is intelligible? Well, it seems to me that here is an appropriate place to bring theology into our multiple layers of explanation.

What kind of answer, after all, can naturalism give to the question of why the universe is intelligible? Keep in mind here the basic tenets of naturalism that I laid out earlier. One of these is that if there's going to be any explanation for anything at all, it has to be a purely naturalistic one. But can naturalism answer coherently the question of why the universe is intelligible at all? Einstein himself would have said no. He insisted that the question of why the universe is comprehensible at all is one that natural science — and by implication naturalism — cannot answer, because science assumes an intelligible universe to begin with. It is the greatest of mysteries that the universe is comprehensible. Clearly then there *are* fundamental facts that lie outside the domain of potential scientific illumination. If naturalism tries to answer our question, the best it can come up with is to say that the universe *just happens* to be intelligible.

I cannot help asking, then, whether this answer provides a good climate in which to do science, especially since science has to presuppose the intelligibility of the universe. Whitehead has also pointed out that it is no accident that science sprouted out of the theologically-shaped Western mind which for centuries had been prepared to assume not only that the universe is intelligible or rational, but that there is a very good reason why the universe is rational, namely, that it is rooted in a divine intelligence.

Once again, in the last example the several levels of explanation do not compete with one another at all. And you can push each level as far as it can possibly go without causing any conflict with the others. So you don't have to say that I am thinking because my neurons are firing *rather than* because I'm trying to understand or *rather than* because the universe is intelligible. Different explanatory levels can exist in harmony, side by side.

To insist that only one level of explanation is enough is called "reductionism." This is not the same as *methodological reduction,* a kind of inquiry essential to science. Methodological reduction would try to explain mind as much as possible in physical terms, but it would not rule out other levels of explanation. As a theologian I am quite content to let science account for mental phenomena in a physical way. For science to do otherwise would be inappropriate.

Reductionism on the other hand, or what is sometimes called *metaphysical reductionism*, is not a method of knowing at all. Rather it is a naturalistic belief, on a par with other beliefs such as those we find in the realm of religion. Metaphysical reductionism, moreover, is a belief that seeks to suppress explanatory pluralism. It is the manifestation of a *will* to squeeze all explanation into a single level, and to deny that anything illuminating can be said at other levels.

Reductionism, to repeat, can best be defined as "the suppression of layered explanation." This is a broader definition of reductionism than the usual, but I prefer it since it acknowledges that theology or any other kind of explanation can be reductionistic too if it refuses to allow for a rich plurality of levels of explanation. For example, theologians and religious people have sometimes thoughtlessly maintained that life came about on earth because of God's creativity *rather than* because of chemical processes. Or they have said that it was divine action *rather than* evolution that brought about human beings. In both examples the questionable assumption is that there can be only one level of explanation and that divine creativity is somehow in competition with natural causes. The way to avoid most problems in science and religion, therefore, is to allow generously for a thickly layered explanation.

What about life?

So, let's come back now to our central question: why did life appear on earth? You will notice that even in science an explanatory pluralism is at work in dealing with this fascinating question. Physics, for example, would explain life in terms of thermodynamics or the self-organizing tendencies of matter. Chemistry — I'm obviously oversimplifying things here — might explain the origin of life in terms of the way carbon bonds with other atoms. Biochemistry would speculate about such possibilities as early RNA replication and many other complex chemical events. My point is simply that there is a kind of explanatory pluralism already operative in the explanation of life even at the level of science itself.

Today, in addition, a new scientific approach has entered into the quest to understand life's origin, namely, astrophysics. It argues that we can't begin to explain how and why life came about on earth without going all the way back to the very opening microseconds of the universe's existence. If life was to come about eventually, certain physical features of the Big Bang universe had to have been "just right" from the very beginning. This point is nicely made by Martin Rees.[16] Rees, a renowned British astronomer, would say that we have to take into account the characteristics of the *whole universe* if we are to make any sense of the origin of life locally. So even in the sciences you can now see a thicker layering of explanation than ever before.

If layered explanation is possible, then it would not be illogical to suppose that there is also room in principle for an ultimate explanation: namely, life also came about because of the attractive power of an infinite generosity. Just as Socrates' sitting in prison may be ultimately explained in terms of the transcendent power of the Good without ruling out physiological accounts of his seated posture, so also it is logically plausible to maintain that the deepest explanation for life's origin is the creative power of God, without denying that chemical and astrophysical factors are also at work in the origin of life. Naturalism, however, supposes that we have to make a choice between such accounts, rather than a layered embrace of many levels simultaneously.

How does theological explanation work?

Imagine that you are scribbling with your pen in a meaningless scrawl on a piece of paper. Then, without lifting your pen from the paper you abruptly start writing a meaningful sentence using letters of the alphabet. From a chemical point of view, that is from the point of view of the chemistry that bonds ink to paper, both types of writing look the same. If the level at which you wish to explain the writing on the page is that of chemistry, you are not going to see anything different in the meaningful sentence from what is taking place in the scribbling. The chemical laws that bind ink to paper are the same in both cases. From a certain point of view, it's all "just a matter of chemistry." But if you've learned how to read, you will be able to see something on the page that a purely chemical approach will miss. You will see letters of a code arranged in a *specific sequence*. There is something informational going on in your meaningful sequence of letters that a chemical analysis of the page alone cannot see.[17]

Let us look closer. You will notice that while you were writing the meaningful informational sequence you violated no physical or chemical laws that had been functioning deterministically while you were merely scribbling. There was no miraculous suspension of the chemical laws that bind ink to paper. Information came onto the page without your interrupting or changing any physical or chemical laws. And yet something powerfully new and significant appeared on the paper, although I could not see it unless I knew how to read. What I'd like to highlight here is how different the page became after the introduction of information, and yet the information entered unobtrusively, in such a way as to change nothing from the perspective of chemistry and physics.

I would suggest that this example provides a useful analogy, though only an analogy, for understanding how divine action may be operative in nature without ever being noticed at purely scientific levels of explanation.

I do not want to suggest that divine action is the direct cause of the specific sequence of letters in segments of DNA that give life an informational character. To link God directly to specific genetic sequences is theologically dangerous and unnecessary. Rather, all I want to point out is that divine action may be *analogous* to informational causality. Information came onto your written page without interrupting anything physically and chemically speaking. Indeed it employed, rather than violated, the chemistry of ink and paper. So also information came into the life process without violating the laws that bind carbon to oxygen, nitrogen, hydrogen and so on.

Information makes all the difference in the world, but it does not disturb anything physically speaking. Information "works" its wonders by way of a gentle and non-intrusive effectiveness. Divine influence, if present to nature at all, would be *analogous* to the non-intrusive effectiveness of information. It would never show up at any of the levels familiar to scientific inquiry. For that reason there should be no competition between scientific and theological explanations of the origin of life. It would be a cheap and crude theology indeed that would try to place divine action at any of the levels of explanation employed by the various sciences. Conversely it is unwarranted for the naturalist to rule out divine influence in nature just because no "evidence" for it appears at the various levels of scientific analysis.

Here we may take a lesson from ancient philosophical Taoism, especially that associated with the Tao Te Ching and its supposed composer Lao-tzu.[18] The idea of a non-interfering kind of causality is a major intuition of this most revered body of ancient teachings. Among the world's great wisdom traditions there is perhaps none that bases itself so squarely on the principle of effective non-intrusiveness as does Taoism. The Tao, the ultimate principle of reality, is said to exercise its influence on nature not by active causation but by *wu-wei*, an untranslatable term for "active inaction" or, as I would prefer, "effective non-interference." In the *Tao Te Ching*, a text attributed to Lao-Tzu (sixth century B.C.) the Tao (or "Way") that moves nature is likened to water, a valley, an uncarved block, or a child. All of these are seen as examples of *wu wei*. They accomplish much while being passive and pliable. In Taoism the universe is governed by non-energetic causation. Common sense and physical science tend to notice things which are prominent and forceful. Lao-Tzu, however, stresses the power of the negative, of that which does not stick out obtrusively. The Tao which shapes nature is so hidden from view that one cannot even name it. It recedes behind or beyond all phenomena and is not to be found among the things which impress our senses. Yet it is all-powerful in its self-withdrawal. Tao is like water:

> That which is best is similar to water.
> Water profits ten thousand things and does not oppose them.
> It is always at rest in humble places that people dislike.
> Thus it is close to Tao (Ch. 8).[19]

The deepest kind of causal influence, according to Lao-Tzu, is non-interference. And the area of our experience governed by force or active energy is superficial in comparison with that shaped by the silent depth of the universe. The Tao is not only non-interfering; it may even be spoken of as "non-being," in the sense that it does not fall among the class of things we normally refer to as "beings." Rather it is "no-thing." And precisely as such it exercises its power to change everything. The *Tao Te Ching* provides these images:

> Thirty spokes are joined at the hub.
> From their non-being arises the function of the wheel.
> Lumps of clay are shaped into a vessel.
> From their non-being arises the functions of the vessel.
> Doors and windows are constructed together to make a chamber.
> From their non-being arises the functions of the chamber.
> Therefore, as individual beings, these things are useful materials.

Constructed together in their non-being, they give rise to function (Ch. 11).

Wu Cheng, a medieval Chinese philosopher, (1249-1333) comments: "If it were not for the empty space of the hub to turn round the wheel, there would be no movement of the cart on the ground. If it were not for the hollow space of the vessel to contain things, there would be no space for storage. If it were not for the vacuity of the room between the windows and doors for lights coming in and going out, there would be no place to live."[20]

I would suggest, then, that divine action, analogous to information, makes itself felt in nature in a comparably non-interfering manner. However, Taoism teaches us that we would be sensitive to such a profound presence only after we have ourselves learned the wisdom of *wu wei* and allowed our lives to be reformed accordingly. Scientific investigation, focusing on the spokes, the clay, the window and door frames, must fall silent when it comes to apprehending the non-intrusive mode of causality that makes things what they are. In Christianity as well as in some other religious traditions there is likewise a fundamental, though often inarticulate conviction that "power is made manifest in weakness." This is one of the central, and one of the most disturbing, insights humans have ever had about the nature of ultimate reality. Taoism expresses it this way:

Gaze at it; there is nothing to see.
It is called the formless.
Heed it; there is nothing to hear.
It is called the soundless.
Grasp it; there is nothing to hold on to.
It is called the immaterial.
Invisible, it cannot be called by any name.
It returns again to nothingness (Ch 14).

The ultimate level of explanation is effective not in spite of but rather because of its non-availability. The intuitions of Taoism (and I think of Christianity and other religious traditions also) render somewhat pretentious the naturalist's demand that all reality show itself as visible evidence. The view that all reality should be subject to our cognitional control is, according to these traditions, a most impoverishing one, rooted in a will to mastery rather than the humble desire to know. Both our senses and our minds need occasionally to look beneath the obviousness of beings.

Numerous colors make man sightless.
Numerous sounds make man unable to hear.
Numerous tastes make man tasteless (Ch. 12).

From the state of being lost in sensations we need to be brought back to a the undifferentiated fullness of ultimate reality.

Contemplate the ultimate void.
Remain truly in quiescence.
All things are together in action,
But I look into their non-action (Ch. 16).

It is not surprising that the idea of non-intrusive effectiveness would be subject to the ridicule of scientific naturalists. To Lao-tzu, however, such ridicule would not be unanticipated:

When a man of superior talent listens to Tao, he earnestly applies it.
When an ordinary man listens to Tao, he seems to believe it and yet
   not to believe it.
When the worst man listens to Tao, he greatly ridicules it.
If he did not ridicule it,
It would not be the Tao (Ch. 41).

Notes

[1] See Charley Hardwick, *Events of Grace: Naturalism, Existentialism, and Theology* (New York: Cambridge University Press,1996).

[2] E. F. Schumacher, *A Guide for the Perplexed (New* York: Harper Colophon Books, 1978), 18ff.

[3] Hans Jonas, *The Phenomenon of Life* (New York: Harper & Row, 1966), p. 9.

[4] Paul Tillich, *Systematic Theology*, Vol. III (Chicago: University of Chicago Press, 1963), p. 19.

[5] Jonas, 9-10.

[6] Ibid.

[7] Jacques Monod, Chance and Necessity, trans. By Austryn Wainhouse (New York: Vintage Books, 1972).

[8] Jonas, 9-10.

[9] Francis H.C. Crick, *Of Molecules and Men* (Seattle: University of Washington Press, 1966), 10.

[10] J. D. Watson, *The Molecular Biology of the Gene* (New York: W.A. Benjamin, Inc.,

1965), 67.

[11] Daniel C. Dennett, *Consciousness Explained* (New York: Little, Brown, 1991), 33.

[12] Owen Flanagan, *The Problem of the Soul: Two Visions of Mind and How to Reconcile Them* (New York: Basic Books, 2002), 167-68.

[13] Alfred North Whitehead, *Process and Reality,* corrected edition, ed. by David Ray Griffin and Donald W. Sherburne (New York: The Free Press, 1978), 162. "It must be remembered that clearness in consciousness is no evidence for primitiveness in the genetic process: the opposite doctrine is more nearly true." (173). We should seek clarity, but then we should mistrust it, since, as Whitehead argues, clarity comes about only as the result of our reading things abstractly. To confuse abstractions with concrete reality is a logical fallacy, the "fallacy of misplaced concreteness." Whitehead thinks that much of modern thought is based on this fallacy. See Alfred North Whitehead, *Science and the Modern World* (New York: The Free Press, 1967), 54-55; 51-57; 58-59.

[14] Plato, *Phaedo,* in *The Last Days of Socrates: Euthyphro, The Apology, Crito, Phaedo,* trans. Hugh Tredennick (New York: Penguin Books, 1969), 156-57.

[15] David Chalmers, "Facing Up to the Problem of Consciousness," *Journal of Consciousness Studies* 2, 1995, 200-219.

[16] Martin Rees, *Our Cosmic Habitat* (Princeton: Princeton University Press, 2001).

[17] Here I am adapting some ideas of Michael Polanyi. See his *Knowing and Being,* ed. by Marjorie Grene (Chicago: University of Chicago Press, 1969); 22-39, 229.

[18] The following paragraphs are adapted from material that I first presented in my book *The Cosmic Adventure* (New York: Paulist Press, 1984).

[19] Excerpts from the Tao Te Ching are those translated by Chang Chung-yuan, *Tao: A New Way of Thinking* (New York: Harper & Row, 1975).

[20] Quoted by Chang Chung-yuan, *Tao: A New Way of Thinking*, 36.

God the Gardener

P. Douglas Kindschi, Ph.D.
Professor of Mathematics and Dean of Science and Mathematics,
Grand Valley State University

Texts: Genesis 2:4b-10
Matthew 13:24-30

Old Testament: The second creation story from Genesis 2 and 3

Genesis 2: 4b - 10. In the day that the LORD God made the earth and the heavens, when no plant of the field was yet in the earth and no herb of the field had yet sprung up — for the LORD God had not caused it to rain upon the earth, and there was no man to till the ground; but a mist went up from the earth and watered the whole face of the ground — then the LORD God formed man of dust from the ground, and breathed into his nostrils the breath of life; and man became a living being.

And the LORD God planted a garden in Eden, in the east; and there he put the man whom he had formed. And out of the ground the LORD God made to grow every tree that is pleasant to the sight and good for food, the tree of life also in the midst of the garden, and the tree of the knowledge of good and evil. A river flowed out of Eden to water the garden, and there it divided and became four rivers.

New Testament: A parable of the kingdom of heaven. Matthew 13

Matt. 13:24-30: Another parable he put before them, saying,

The kingdom of heaven may be compared to a man who sowed good seed in his field; but while men were sleeping, his enemy came and sowed weeds among the wheat, and went away. So when the plants came up and bore grain, then the weeds appeared also. And the servants of the householder came and said to him, "Sir, did you not sow good seed in your field? How then has it weeds?" He said to them, "An enemy has done this." The servants said to him, "Then do you want us to go and gather them?" But he said, "No; lest in gathering the weeds you root up the wheat along with them. Let both grow together until the harvest; and at harvest time I will tell the reapers, Gather the weeds first and bind them in bundles to be burned, but gather the wheat into my barn."

The Bible speaks in metaphors, images, poetry and parables. Especially when trying to describe God, our human language is stretched and is finally inadequate to express that which is so far beyond the ability of our words to describe. And so the Bible talks about God as light, fortress, father, mother, shepherd, potter, judge and king. We often talk about God as king, creator, all powerful, and there are certainly good reasons to do so. The first chapter of Genesis uses this kingly language when describing the act of creation. God speaks and it is so. His mere word brings about the sun, the moon and stars. A word is given and plants and animals appear. The Creator says: "Let the earth bring forth living creatures of every kind: cattle and creeping things, and wild animals of the earth of every kind." And it is so. It certainly brings about a sense of awe and realization of the power and transcendence of our God.

This image of God was greatly reinforced by the scientific developments of the 17th Century with Newton and the mechanistic model for the universe. God, the creator, became God the engineer, the designer of the universe. As our scientific theories became more mathematical we had pictures of God the geometer. Scientists believed they were finding the mind of God as they discovered beautiful, mathematical descriptions of the natural world. Even the artists pictured God with a compass laying out the world at creation. This mechanical model for the universe took hold as the predominate picture for the natural order. God was often seen as this engineer-creator. One who not only created the universe, but also created the laws by which this universe would run. In my own Presbyterian tradition, there was a time when God was not only seen as the all-powerful creator, but was also all-determining. Not only did God create the world, God also controlled every atom, every event, every minute thing that ever happens.

While this mechanical image of the universe may have made sense in a Newtonian world it no longer works for a physics with quantum indeterminacy. It doesn't fit an evolutionary biology based on random mutations and adaptation to changing environments. Furthermore, it doesn't even fit our theology of a God who desires good for us but does not take away our freedom and turn us into automatons. Control might not be the only or the best image for how God works in our lives and in our world. Perhaps we need to return to the biblical sources to rediscover the earlier images of a God who shepherds, who plants, who nurtures.

In this second creation story found in Genesis 2, which we read this morning, we see an earlier account from the Yahweh source that presents a very different image for God. Here we see a God who plants a garden, causes trees to grow, and sees that they are watered. God forms Adam from the dust of the ground and breathes "into his nostrils the breath of life." God forms the animals and brings them to Adam to name. In an anesthetic "deep sleep" Adam's rib is removed and formed into Eve. God walks in the garden in the cool of the day. This is a gardener God.

Before I go on, let me first make a confession. I am not a gardener, but I am married to one and so I know a little about how gardening works.

First, a gardener doesn't control every aspect of her creation. Plants do not always appear where and how it was intended. Sometimes a seed will be carried by the wind or a bird to a different place and the next year a plant will grow in a new location. She calls them volunteers. Sometimes the root system gets too crowded and the plant needs to be dug up, separated and replanted as two or more plants. Weeds sprout up. Soil conditions and weather enter into the process. Some plants seem to have free will. No matter what you think you are intending, they just do their own thing. The gardener's job is to nurture, shape and care.

Second, gardening takes time. When we put in a new pergola in our side yard six years ago, my wife planted the vines that would cover the structure. I thought it would give us the shade we had hoped for yet that year. Now six years later the vines have finally reached the top and are beginning to create the desired cover. She tells me that gardeners must be patient. Gardening has been described as the art form that requires the longest time to create. It takes hard work, constant effort, and most of all patience to shape and form the contours and colors desired.

Third, a garden is never finished; it is always in process. There is always more to do. It is a dynamic art form. It is not like painting a picture and at some point you are done. It is not like a poem that has a beginning and an end. It is not a symphony that can be heard in one night's concert. It is always becoming, always being developed, always in process.

Do these characteristics of gardening describe God's relationship to our world and even to our own lives? Do we have a God who nurtures and cares for us and for the creation? Does the working of God's will often take time, more time than our impatient desires would expect? Is God's work in the world and in our lives a work in progress, and not yet finished?

This gardening image is found in the New Testament as well. When Christ speaks of the "kingdom of God" it is not a royal kingdom that is described but more likely the image of a vineyard, of the weeds growing along with the wheat, and of the seeds falling on different kinds of soil. In describing the early church in Corinth, the Apostle Paul says that he planted and Apollos watered, "but God gave the growth."

Brian Austin in his book *The End of Certainty and the Beginning of Faith*, tells of hiking with his family along the trails which parallel stream beds in the Great Smoky Mountains. They often returned with mud caked hiking boots. While he finds himself impressed with the majesty of the mountains, it is also, (in his words), "the mud, still glistening with the mist that makes dust come to life [that] harbors mysteries as magnificent as the mountains.... From that mud, from its carbon, nitrogen, hydrogen, oxygen, and assorted metals, a child can be woven. The atoms in that mud, the same kinds of atoms that comprise my children and you and me, have existed for billions of years....Jesus the Christ, in whom God was reconciling the world to God's self, was made of those same kinds of atoms, very old atoms. This muddy clay is no trivial, commonplace annoyance. This mud is spectacular, and we believe that God made it so. This mud is rich, pregnant with possibility. It is worthy of God's becoming, in Jesus, a mudball like us. This is the incarnation, God become mudball. To see ourselves as made of the same stuff that rests under our boots as we journey a mountain path is no insult to human dignity, no affront to the image of God in us; it is rather a reminder of the majesty of inspired mud, a reflected majesty that gives us but one more fleeting glimpse of the blinding brilliance of the maker of the mud" (149-150).

Yes, we are God-breathed dust, mudballs in the image of God, clay in the hands of the potter. We live in a garden, not a perfectly designed machine. Our world has a place for chance, for random events, and for freedom. We live in a garden, but not in a wilderness. The chaotic forces are here, but not in control. There is a gardener who prunes and shapes; a gardener who nurtures and cares. It takes time, sometimes more time than we would like. Weeds grow around us, but it is not yet time for the harvest when the weeds and the wheat will be separated. It is dynamic and not finished. Our world, our lives, even our ideas are not completed. We are in process and the one who cares, who nurtures, is having influence on this process. The gardener is as work.

As we seek to understand God in new ways, as we strive to rediscover images of God that make sense in this scientific yet postmodern world, we might find that image in the nurturing, caring, and even pruning activity of the gardener.

In this Lenten season we focus on the last days of Christ. We see him praying in the **Garden** of Gethsemane, we find him placed in a tomb in the **garden** which belongs to Joseph of Arimathea. It is in that garden that Mary Magdalene visits the tomb but finds it empty. In John 20 we read:

But Mary stood weeping outside the tomb. As she wept, she bent over to look into the tomb; and she saw two angels in white, sitting where the body of Jesus had been lying... They said to her, "Woman, why are you weeping?" She said to them, "They have taken away my Lord, and I do not know where they have laid him." When she had said this, she turned around and saw Jesus standing there, but she did not know that it was Jesus. Jesus said to her, "Woman, why are you weeping? Whom are you looking for?" Supposing him to be the **gardener**, she said to him, "Sir, if you have carried him away, tell me where you have laid him, and I will take him away." [Then] Jesus said to her, "Mary!" She turned and said to him in Hebrew, "Rabbouni!" (which means Teacher)....Then Mary Magdalene went and announced to the disciples, "I have seen the Lord."

This morning, we began in the Garden of Eden where the creator is portrayed as one who plants a garden and breaths life into that which has been formed from the dust and mud of the earth. A caring, nurturing God seeks not to control but to empower, to shape and influence, while respecting the freedom and independence of that which is created. Our exploration has now taken us to another garden, the garden of the empty tomb. It is here that we, along with Mary Magdalene, see the risen Christ as the gardener. In our own world we have moved beyond that mechanical image of nature and can see anew the wisdom of the biblical images. We can discover again a God who appears in the image of a gardener.

Discussions

The discussions are the core of the conference. Here the participants have the opportunity to pursue the issues in detail in directions of their own choosing. The discussions are then not easily divided into direct responses to the issues raised in the lectures. Certain broad subject-areas can be detected in the topics discussed. These form the headings into which the discussions have been divided here. Under each of these headings the discussions have been divided chronologically into the session in which each discussion occurred. This allows the reader to follow the progression of the ideas through the conference and their development as Professor Haught developed his ideas through the lectures. Professor Haught's responses often indicate that the subject of a question will be developed in his next lecture.

The Persons raising questions or issues are identified by a questioner number. The list of the individuals is available to conference participants on request.

The discussions are divided into the following headings

1. Cosmic purpose
2. Scientific methodology
3. Evolution and Darwinism

4. Evolution and the Soul
5. Chaos and Complexity
6. Love, Suffering and Power

Each of these has been subdivided into the specific topics covered in the separate discussions. The topics in the discussions were not limited. Therefore the editorial divisions are somewhat arbitrary. In the editing of these the substance of the question asked has been shortened to make the issue clear. Professor Haught's responses are given in their entirety.

Cosmic purpose
a. What purpose?
b. New Heavens/New Earth
c. Creation
d. God's Omnipotence/Benevolence
e. Freedom and Creation
f. Cosmic Time-Scales
g. Time and Eternity

What Purpose?

Friday Evening

[Questioner 1] All this process of complexification toward the noosphere implies an increasing amount of change and progress toward the higher level. However, around volume 37 or 38 as you have presented them, when the sun becomes a giant red star, all of this will disappear completely. So what happens then to all that has been developed?

[Haught] Well, the reason I came to this conference is to find the answer to that question, with all these experts here [laughter]. And so I'd like to know what the answer to that question is. That's something I hope we can talk about in the next couple days because that's a very, very good question. I have my ideas on it. Most of you are going to be around for the discussions tomorrow, so why don't we bring that up in our conversations, and I would really like to hear what other people think of that.

Do let me rephrase the question. I've talked to you about the plausibility of cosmic purpose. But almost inevitably someone will and should raise the question that you just raised. If the universe as a whole, and I shall make it a little bit more catastrophic than you did, even, is going to freeze or fry, as they say, then what possible point can we attribute to it? Surely if there is going to be a point to it there has to be some way in which the value that has been realized in the universe — and I have defined purpose as the realization of value — is saved or redeemed eternally. If that is not available, then this is not a purposive universe. For this universe to be purposive, the value that it has achieved has to be the product of some transcendent intentionality. But it also has to be something that somehow can be rescued from the abyss of nothingness.

So theology, in its confrontation with science, has to address that question. I hope that we can talk about it. I'd like to get your own thoughts on this in the next couple of days. My own approach would be pretty much Whiteheadian. In my own quest to understand the relationship between science and religion I turn to Whitehead's thought because I think he has the categories to deal with that. But I don't think you find those in traditional theology. We didn't have this sense of the wide, evolving universe. But I think that is a question that we should talk about. Thank you for bringing it up.

New Heavens/ New Earth

Friday Evening

[Questioner 2] Scripture promises new heavens and a new earth. Can this be reconciled with the idea that the universe is evolving towards either higher forms of beauty or Teilhard's omega point? Is the universe evolving towards that final state of perfection, that shalom, that eternal bliss, or will there be a sort of discontinuity? Some Christian traditions emphasize the discontinuity, which in its most vulgar form claims that the world will be destroyed anyway so we should just save souls. How much of what we used to call heaven is a continuation of this universe? How much of a qualitative change should we think about?

[Haught] That is an excellent question. And, of course, I'm not in a position, nor is any of us in a position, to answer that with any great clarity. What I would say, though, is this. It seems to me incoherent to deny some continuity between the world as we experience it now and the world as it is promised to us eschatologically. If that is the case, then the promise that you were talking about would probably, it seems to me, make no sense. Because what would happen, if you have the completely discontinuous scenario, is that this present world and everything that it stood for will be totally destroyed, annihilated, and another will take its place. Now, I don't personally see the scriptures, or the tradition as I understand it, opting for that radical discontinuity at all.

So what we have (and this is part of the whole problem of science and religion) is that our religious traditions have been shaped according to, I think, the optimism-of-withdrawal scenario that Teilhard talks about. This world will end, and it doesn't really matter, because our souls will survive and be taken off into the Platonic world of heaven, as it were. I don't see this dualism in the Bible. I don't see that really as the central biblical instinct, or the Christian instinct. I can understand why Christian hope, when it came into the Greek world, would be translated into that idiom. But it seems to me that the fundamental biblical instinct is that creation is good, and if it is good, intrinsically good, then its absolute annihilation, and the creation of something new in its place, doesn't seem to me to follow, at least not from the biblical perspective.

I'll talk a little more about this tomorrow. I think that what we have to do when we think about the universe from a biblical point of view, is emphasize the theme of promise. If there's any motif in the Bible that ties that strange body of books together, it's the idea that God is one who makes promises. And a promise is something that is present here and now, that is to be nourished here and now. And that promise is somehow continuous with its fulfillment, or else, it seems that the Biblical way of looking at things doesn't make any sense at all. It collapses into a kind of dualism. So I can't be more specific about that except to say that I can't help trusting, if you will, that what we are doing here on earth matters. And the way I would put it is very close to the way Teilhard puts it: that there is no such thing as a heaven apart from a renewed earth. I would extend that now to a renewed cosmos.

There are other ways you can deal with this, too. From a Whiteheadian point of view the universe is not a collection of particles. It is a story. It is a process which is decomposable into events or happenings. Whitehead's disciple Charles Hartshorne talks a lot about this and how the characteristic of events is to accumulate.

Particles dissolve and disappear. But happenings keep adding up. So, Whitehead's notion of God as one who takes into the divine life the whole series of events that make up the universe, seems to me to be one that's very consistent with the notion of resurrection as well. I think there is continuity. There's discontinuity within continuity, but it's not absolute discontinuity.

Creation

Saturday Afternoon

[Questioner 3] Where do we see the hope for the future? Within my own understanding there is the hope for the continuation of the kingdom of heaven, the new heaven and new earth, and beyond that. Where is the connection of God to creation?

[Haught] Traditionally, theology talks about the doctrine of creation in three chapters. There is *creatio originalis*, original creation, which was, and I guess still is for most people, the paradigmatic view of creation. Something happened back there in the beginning. But there has also been, almost from the beginning of Christian theology, the notion of *creatio continua*, that God's concursus is essential to keep the universe in being. God is eternally, continually creating. And then there is *creatio nova*, the eschatological fulfillment of creation. These three moments are part of the Christian theology.

Creatio continua was not emphasized traditionally nearly as much as it has since Darwin, since we became aware of evolution as the process of on-going creation. And who can say much about *Creatio nova*?

God's Omnipotence/Benevolence

Saturday Morning

[Questioner 4] When considering process theology I find it necessary to balance God's omnipotence with God's benevolence. There has to be some degree of holding back. I sometimes get the uneasy feeling that the God of process theology — and this is more of a feeling than a thought — is kind of an impotent, whimpering God. He's the fellow sufferer, sort of like Bill Clinton, he feels our pain, he cries, he bites his lip, but claims, "I can't do a whole lot about it." And so I was wondering if we could have some conversation about

the notion of divine authority and power, and how they are manifested in this dynamic universe.

[Haught] I'll discuss this a bit more in my talk this morning. But
it seems to me that one way in which you can understand Christianity is that it brought about — or at least it should have brought about
— a revolution in the whole idea of what power is. I'm not sure that
we have yet caught up with this. Whitehead himself is famous for
saying that when Christianity entered the West, Caesar conquered.
In other words, we came in our liturgy, in our art, and in our theology, to model God after the potentate, the Caesar, the dictator. You
can see this in a lot of mosaics after the Constantinian era, and you
can see it in a lot of theology. And the humble shepherd of Nazareth, upon whom Christianity originally modeled its understanding of God, has receded into the background. I think that one of the
reasons many Christian theologians were somewhat captivated by
the process idea, is that it does tend, more than many other frameworks, to allow a notion of power that is able to accommodate the
primordial Christian imagery of the crucified God and the humble
shepherd of Nazareth. So I think your question is: how could that
kind of notion of power really be the effective, salvific and redemp-
tive sort of power that we need and that we look for. You referred to
this image as that of a whimpering God. Certainly it seems to me
that Christianity introduces the idea of the vulnerability of deity
into the picture. The Marduks, the Jupiters, all these, as the great
English theologian, John MacQuarrie, says, recede into the background in Christianity. And the God of Christianity is one who shares
in our sufferings, and shares in our weaknesses as well.

But that does raise your question, and maybe this is something
that all of us could talk about. How can we still refer to this as power?
And in Christianity we are instructed not to think of divine power
independently of divine love. So in some sense, the issue comes down
to the question: in what sense is love powerful, especially if love is
also vulnerable? If love is vulnerable, even unto death, how could
we call that powerful? Well, I think we have answered this by defining what we mean by power. The way I would understand it, and I
think this is the way some process theologians understand it, is that
power fundamentally means the capacity to influence.

If you are talking about beings which don't have much internal
freedom or subjectivity or interiority to them, then inanimate things

like rocks can be influenced by a coercive type of power. But when you are talking about beings which have an internal dimension of indeterminacy or freedom or subjectivity to them — and for Whitehead, you have to remember, that is everything since every actual entity is a subject — the situation is different. You can't really influence these subjects, unless somehow the subjects internalize your effective presence as power. How do you get inside subjects to influence them? Not by coercion, but by persuasion. In that sense persuasion is not a whimpering type of power. It is the most effective way in which beings, especially endowed with subjectivity, are influenced. And as subjectivity intensifies in the evolving universe, and the subjectivity takes on the form of what we call human freedom, the issue becomes: how does power influence freedom? And, at least in the Christian perspective, we have freedom. My response would be that freedom is influenced much more effectively by a persuasive, vulnerable, self-suffering, compassionate reality, than by a miracle-working, intervening deity who manipulates matter in accordance with what I consider to be a rather immature will on our part.

So those are just some thoughts. There is a lot more to be said.

Freedom and Creation

Saturday Afternoon

[Questioner 4] Can you speak more to the idea that a perfect cosmos would by definition be an extension of the creator.

[Haught] What I said was "an initially completed cosmos would be an extension of the creator."

[Questioner 4] I am not capable of producing a perfect anything. If I were that would be an extension of me, although it would not be me. Eschatologically if all things are made whole, if there were no more crying and the lion lay down with the lamb, would that be an appendage of God? Or would it be something that has its own identity?

[Haught] The category that you have left out is freedom. A world that has intensity of being to it, I think we could argue philosophically and theologically, would be a world in which there are the conditions for the actualization of freedom, and that freedom would be other than the divine. I have not worked this out, but it is certainly worth thinking about. It seems to me that the things that go on in evolution, that are so troubling to us initially, have some intrinsic connection with the fact that the world is one that promotes emergent freedom. If you are going to extrapolate from that emergent freedom to an eschatological extension of that emergent freedom, then the final state or condition is not one in which things are exactly related to one another as a kind of extension of God's own being, but one in which the world achieves, in the presence of the divine, a maximum degree of otherness. Then, and this is the beauty of it, a genuine dialog becomes possible.

God wants a dialogical world, a world that can converse with the divine, rather than a world that is just a puppet, just a marionette, on the divine strings that control it. Such a condition would not be a static one. Rather, as I mentioned earlier with reference to Karl Rahner's categories of the infinite and the finite, the freedom would still be a finite freedom in the presence of the infinite freedom. Perhaps it would be a much more animated and aesthetically intense reality than what we have now. Certainly we are not there yet. So let's hope that something in the way of an intensification of freedom would emerge eschatologically that will not be an extension of the divine. An instantaneously perfected world would not have the opportunity to become itself. It seems to me that there is something dramatically beautiful about a world that is allowed to become itself in the presence of God. That is the great gift that Darwin has given us, theologically.

Cosmic Time Scales

Saturday Morning

[Questioner 3] Last night we talked about Teilhard's overview of development, the cosmos over time, and then the geosphere on to the noosphere. Thinking in terms of a hope for greater consciousness and complexity it seems that we could look at it on many scales. But it is not just the larger scale, but also on the smaller scale, beyond the Planck length. Maybe something is happening on those smaller scales, which we can't say too much about. But does that seem to fit within your understanding of Teilhard, to emphasize both the within and without?

[Haught] Very much so. Thank you. His thought moves between two poles. There is the pole of multiplicity, and fragmentation, and individuality at the bottom; and the pole of unity, consciousness, and spirit at the top. And his thought is that there is no such thing as matter. Matter is a tendency in the universe toward fragmentation and multiplicity. Another way in which he puts it is to say that matter is spirit in the state of multiplicity. What he wants us to allow for is — and it really comes down essentially to this — that the present state of the universe in which we find ourselves is not to be taken as final. One thing seems clear, and this is where science really does help us. Science has helped us to realize that the universe has made what Teilhard calls progress, and by progress he means advances in complexity and consciousness. Who of us, if we had been present say a hundred or so years after the Big Bang, looking out at that massive sea of radiation, which was the universe in a state of dispersal, would have seen any promise in it. But time, evolution and some favoring divine presence, in Teilhard's view, have brought about those incredible, new, novel breakthroughs that have occasionally taken place after long, long periods of gestation and waiting. Who of us would have ever predicted, then, that out of this would come the great beauty and diversity of life, of consciousness, of science, and of religion.

Something has been happening. This is comparable to the way the Bible works. The Bible tells stories of God's great acts in the past. Why? Because these stories give us a sense that there is still a future. I think that is why Teilhard tells the story of nature. He's a paleontologist, and paleontologists dwell in the past. But as he grew older he became increasingly dissatisfied with these journeys into the past. I think in terms of your powers of ten he would have said, "OK, let's go back to the infinitesimal, but then let's turn back toward the future." He said that he was a journeyer to the past who became a pilgrim of the future. And that's how he wants us to look at what has happened in the past, as a reason for hoping in the present, that it is not over.

Teilhard did not believe that the shear force of the noosphere is itself enough for us to trust that a next stage of consciousness is going to happen because it is inevitable. At the human level there also has to be a force of attraction that pulls things together. It is analogous to the force of attraction in the strong — weak nuclear force and in gravity. At the human level, the level of the noosphere, the force of attraction has to be that of love. And it is here that he saw the evolutionary role of religion. Religion provides first a great hope held in common. But it also encourages us, not just Christianity, but other religions, too, to love one another. That will be the necessary glue or force of attraction that would allow for any further emergence in cosmic evolution.

Time and Eternity

Saturday Afternoon

[Questioner 5] I believe that God's relation to time is very important to theological questions as well as theology and science. I was wondering if the views that you presented necessitate a certain view of God's relation to time, and if so, or if not, would you comment a little bit on what some of the ramifications are?

[Haught] When you talk about time, you leave me behind. Of course the great mystery from Augustine to Einstein is time. The only things that I could say are very general. I would like to see God not so much outside of time as inclusive of time. That, I think, is implied already in St. Paul's sermon in Acts. There Paul refers to God as the one in whom we live and move and have our being. I think you could extend that to the whole universe. God is the one in whom the whole universe lives and moves and has its being as well. So God is not separate from time. But God is *distinct* from time. There must be an eternal aspect, a timeless aspect of God, in so far as God is the reservoir of all the possibilities that could be realized in time. But God is also temporal in a sense that I talked about this morning in terms of the dipolar understanding of God. Precisely because God is absolutely related to everything, God would be absolutely related to time as well.

Let me talk a little about absolute relatedness. In classical theism, a big question came up as to whether we could think of God if God is omnipotent, omniscient, eternal, and immutable. If God is what classical theology thought God was, how could God in any way be related to the world? By relating God to the world aren't we jeopardizing divine transcendence, bringing it down to our level, as it were? And so there was a strong temptation, in Aquinas and others, to teach that God is not related internally to the world.

The question I think we have to ask today — not only because of Darwin and evolution, but simply for religious reasons — is: "What kind of images of God are projected if we think conceptually in terms of God as not related?" So what we have to do, I think, is to be faithful to the tradition that God is not in any way jeopardized, in God's eternal essence, by what happens in the vicissitudes of history and the crazy things that go on in this world. So the way to do that — and again this is Schubert Ogden's way, and also Charles Hartshorne's way — is to think of God's absoluteness as *absolute relatedness*. To draw that out a bit, consider that a rock is related to its environment in a rather minimal sort of way. A plant, speaking hierarchically, seems to be more intimately related to its environment, to the ground that it emerges from. An animal can move around and relate to a lot more environmentally than a rock or a plant. So why can't we think of God, analogously to that relatedness, as the absolutely related One?

God relates to everything. So you are preserving the notion of God's absoluteness, eternity and immutability at one pole of the divine being, while at the other pole you are allowing for God's relatedness, God's experience of the temporality of the world, without that in any way eliminating God's absoluteness and eternity. And I think that is religiously more compatible with the Biblical idea. The Bible believes in a responsive God. God is not aloof from history and time, but God enters into time, takes time into the divine life. So that is how I would deal with it.

Scientific Methodology

a. Materialism
b. Methodological Materialism
c. Methodological Naturalism
d. Matter
e. Classical Method
f. Scientific Objectivity
g. Scientific Separation
h. Science Without Faith
i. Values in Science
j. Layered Explanation

Materialism

Friday Evening

[Questioner 6] I agree with you very strongly that purpose and teleology are correct and important, and I wonder whether you have been in conversation with biologists, who are disciples of Jacques Monod or Richard Dawkins. If you have, what do you say?

[Haught] This is one of the biggest questions in science and religion today. I think that some of the ideas of these biologists come less from their biology than from their ideology. They have certain assumptions about the nature of reality that they find convenient to organize mentally for themselves, producing a sort of ideology. This ideology is physicalist or materialist — there are different names for it. Whitehead called it scientific materialism. I still think that the best response to scientific materialism is in Whitehead's *Science and the Modern World*[1]. In the chapter dealing with the 17th century, he says that the whole modern world has been based upon abstractions. We've taken the primary qualities, the measurable qualities of things, out of what William James called the "booming, buzzing confusion of the universe." We've focused on those so much, that we've forgotten that they are abstractions from the very complex, organismic world that we all are part of.

It's very difficult to respond to these people by giving them a course in Whitehead, because they don't have the time or the patience for it. But often people who have taken the time do realize the logical error here, or what I think is a logical error, and that's the confusion of concrete reality with the mental abstraction. They take the mental abstraction to be concrete reality. That has become, as some have termed it — Whitehead is not the only one to point this out — the metaphysical foundation of modern science. I'll talk about this on Sunday. Paul Tillich refers to this as an ontology of death. We've taken stuff which is intrinsically dead, or made to seem like it's dead, and then tried methodologically to account for life and mind in terms of stuff that's dead. Well, Whitehead would say that it was never dead to begin with. The deadness is due to abstractions that we thought were concrete reality.

There are other ways to deal with it as well. Maybe I can talk more about this tomorrow. What these people have done is to treat chance and necessity as though they were concrete realities. I think those are also abstractions. Chance is a word that we confuse with the openness of the universe to the future. For the universe to be open to the future it has to percolate with contingency. Otherwise it would be dead and frozen. Necessity, it seems to me, is an exaggeration of a feature of this universe that I would call consistency, and in that consistency there is an openness. The universe is not reducible to necessity and chance.

Methodological Materialism

Saturday Afternoon

[Questioner 7] In this morning's presentation you made a strong statement against materialism. Does a scientist need to be a methodological materialist? Is there a way that science can proceed on a non-materialist methodology, making a distinction, obviously, between the ontological commitment and the methodological? And then you made a distinction between the creator and the creation. Yet, as I understand, much process thought tends to have a panentheist understanding, in which there is a closer tie between God and the world. I'd like to have you speak to that point as well.

[Haught] I don't know whether you are familiar with David Griffin, the process theologian. He makes a lot of the need to revise the whole notion of what science is in the light of evolution and new scientific discoveries, including parapsychology, which he has gotten into recently. He believes science should include the discussion of things that it has traditionally left out.

My own instinct, especially as far as the science-theology dialog is concerned, is, as I said before, to let science be science. Let it be methodologically materialist. Let it be methodologically physicalist. Let it even be methodologically atheist, if you want, in the sense that science gets very uncomfortable if it has to bring talk of the divine into its discourse. I think that I would like to respect that. I would compare science to something like a game of soccer. I am not trying to demean it in any way. But when we go out onto the field to play soccer, we decide that we are not going to use our hands. We are going to see what we can accomplish athletically by using our feet. It turns out that you can do quite a bit. You can focus life very interestingly in that way.

Likewise science decides that when we examine the world we are not going to bring in ideas about God, final cause, meaning, intentionality and subjectivity, purpose, or value. We are going to leave all those out, and see what we can find by focusing on nature in that way. Personally I think that it is fine to be aware that you are using a self-restricting kind of method, something like in a game. But when you come off the soccer field, and you are eating supper, you are allowed to use your hands again. So, when you come off the scientific field, it seems appropriate to bring in things you left out while you were doing science.

So I think the big controversy is, in many ways, not between science and theology. The controversy is between the belief that the self-restricting and successful method called science is really the only way in which we should approach the real world, and the belief that those other approaches that argue for many layers of under-standing and explanation. There is the big divide between the ex-planatory monists and the explanatory pluralists, but not between science and theology.

That is an answer that is probably going to be too glib for a lot of people. But I found that it is not helpful in the science and religion dialog to expect science to break out of its traditional ways of look-ing at things. I think that the conversation works better if you do not ask for this.

Methodological Naturalism

Saturday Afternoon

[Questioner 7] You distinguish, then, your position from peo-ple who believe that science should not be committed exclusively to methodological naturalism.

[Haught] Yes. Some people think that methodological natural-ism is the slippery slope to metaphysical naturalism. Well, I sup-pose it can be very tempting for a certain kind of personality. But logically speaking I think that the distinctions are clear and crisp. Maybe, psychologically speaking, some people who get into meth-odological naturalism end up in metaphysical naturalism. But in order to prevent that I think all you have to do is just be aware of these distinctions that I am talking about. Again, that might be too simple an answer, but I think it works. At least it works as a starting point in science and religion conversation.

Matter

Saturday Afternoon

[Questioner 8] My son had a football coach as a science teacher in eighth grade. The first question on a physics test was, "What is matter?" He had been given a definition to memorize, which was something like "the material component of all elements," or some equally circular and vague description. I tried to explain to him, probably no more clearly, that matter itself is a metaphysical term. We don't know what matter is, or matter/energy. Those are all our attempts, I think, as more contemporary philosophers of science would put it, to focus in on the most general concepts under which we try to understand things.

This approach has led to a dead kind of world in which the machine metaphor is more than a metaphor. So when somebody is going to be methodologically naturalistic, are they just choosing a different fundamental organizing scheme than someone who would do otherwise? But if nature is not enough, in the end can we not say that the nature of God is not enough either?

[Haught] I agree with you that we still don't know what matter is. And we don't know what nature is. But science has a pretty well-defined method of looking at things. So maybe we could provisionally define the material world as that world that is the objective of scientific enquiry and scientific method, which is defined by the method itself. I'm a Lonerganian, in many ways. I cut my theological teeth on Bernard Lonergan and his notion of truth-seeking and reality. He defines being, for example, as the objective of the pure, unrestricted desire to know. In other words, an epistemic way of looking at things in a sense circumscribes what you mean by the object of that kind of enquiry. Science has a specific kind of method, which uses observation, which is what we can detect through our senses. It doesn't go as far as Whitehead would allow inquiry to go, to talk about things which our deeper perceptive apparatus, deeper than the senses, is able to put us in touch with. That is left out of science. Because of that we end up in science with a rather restricted set of objects of its enquiry.

So I would understand the material/physical world in that general sort of sense. But that does not give you a metaphysically satisfying answer to the question of matter. Now if we are going to understand matter, even within science, we have to take into account the outcomes of the movement of matter in evolution. Some of those outcomes have subjectivity and consciousness. Some suggest that we need to widen our understanding of what science is. But scientific method is deliberately self-limiting. I am willing to go along with that self-limitation of method when we talk about the objective of science.

Let me just come back to the second point that you made. First of all I don't try to be consistent with every aspect of process theology. I am very eclectic. However, I think you can talk about panentheism as John Polkinghorne does. I am inclined right now to think of what he calls eschatological panentheism as a nice framework for science and theology. By that he means that because the world is not yet finished, the world is still becoming itself, and that what we hope for is that the world will be fully taken into the divine life. But I doubt that we must say here and now that the world is fully congruent with the internal feelings of the divine. There is a kind of epistemic distance as well as a theological distance, at least from the point of view of the world. From God's point of view, of course, everything is already included. But from the point of view of the world, we are not quite where we could be, we are not finished, the world is not yet complete.

Classical Method

Friday Evening

[Questioner 9] The classical, scientific method, which is to observe, form a hypothesis that can be tested, and tests it experimentally, has worked very well going down your hierarchical chain, trying to explain how small things finally fit together to become the universe as we understand it. It is not clear that this is going to work if we attempt to look up the chain to the next emergence. Many scientific problems are too complex for the formulation of single testable hypotheses. How can we understand a universe that is so complex? Can you give some insight into how the scientific method of thinking about things is going to have to change to contribute to the way you are envisioning science and religion fitting together?

[Haught] Well, that's a very good question, too. The short answer is that I prefer to let science be science and to let it deal with what you call stuff that's lower in the chain. You are sort of assuming a hierarchical view of things, which I think we all take implicitly. Even evolutionists assume a kind of chain of being in the way they think of things. I don't want to burden science with trying to answer questions which are off its radar screen. At this time, unfortunately, in our philosophy departments as well as in popular expressions of science, a lot of the so-called pundits and experts in science, do hold forth on questions such as meaning and purpose and so forth, as though these are questions that science itself is able to deal with.

My own position is that we should not burden science with the types of inquiry that are just too large for it. I honestly think, and probably a lot of you do too, that there are just a lot of things for which scientific method, as it's being carved out in modern times, is simply inadequate. I would bring up again the notion of *adaequatio*.[2] To me it seems that this is a fundamental theme that has disappeared from many science and religion conversations. To make our minds proportionate to the kind of realities that grasp hold of us we have to undergo a kind of surrender that the scientific mind does not have to undergo, and should not be expected to undergo. Science, it seems to me, does rightly look for a kind of objective mastery of its field. But there are indeed aspects of reality that cannot be approached with the epistemic stance of objectification or mastery. I think this is true even in our ordinary experience. Other persons cannot be approached that way. To become adequate to the reality of other persons, such as the one you love, you have to go through a personal transformation. So why wouldn't that be all the more the case with dimensions of reality which are more important than even persons in our own experience. So I think we have to be fair to science and not burden it with trying to make excursions into territory that it should not be at home in.

However, after saying that, I don't fall into, as most of you know, the separatist or independence position which claims that science deals with one thing, and that it can't conflict with religion because religion deals with something else. After making these distinctions

I want to say, like the medieval philosophers, that we distinguish in order to relate. So, I do think, along with Holmes Rolston, III, that science places constraints on what we can plausibly say about ultimate reality and about purpose and meaning and so forth. Even though it can't answer those questions directly, it does limit what we say theologically and remain plausible. You'll see this in my talk tomorrow. I think that after Darwin we simply cannot have exactly the same thoughts about God that we had before. A lot of people don't like that idea, but I'm excited about it.

Scientific Objectivity

Saturday Afternoon

[Questioner 10] I think that God's only way to find out about his world is science. We just don't have any other means to get at it. I think that when you go to beauty, love, and all these kinds of things as explanations, that's fiction. I don't like the soccer metaphor.

[Haught] Even within our own experience we have different fields through which the desire to know travels. We can't really allow ourselves to grasp the reality of deity unless we take a somewhat different route from the one that science takes. We can't grasp the interpersonal reality of those that we contact, unless we use some other method of inquiry than just pure, detached, disinterested scientific objectification. We can learn a lot about reality through telling stories that we can't learn in any other way. So there is a narrative field, an aesthetic field, and there's an interpersonal field. We have this unrestricted desire to know, but to channel it all through the method of objectification that science uses and to say that that is the only way that we can really come in touch with reality, is going to lead us eventually to what I think you yourself said, namely, that everything else like beauty will look like a fiction that we impose upon the real world, which we have identified on the basis of scientific method.

I know that a lot of people would agree with you on that, but I don't. I don't think we do justice to the human capacity to put ourselves in touch with reality if we limit it only to the theoretic field, or the scientific method of encounter with reality. I think there are a lot of different ways that we can get in touch with things.

As I said earlier, I think there are deeper ways of perception than just sense perception. Whitehead has pointed out often that our sense perception of the world, which is vital to science, is really already an abstraction from a more fundamental way of coming into encounter with reality, through our whole being. He distinguishes between sense perception and perception in the mode of causal efficacy. In the latter we somehow feel ourselves being created at a very deep level by the cosmic process. The universe impacts us viscerally, and not just cognitionally. It is true that in modern thought our senses have been taken as the foundational point of entry into reality. But the five senses are really already abstracting from a more fundamental mode of encounter with reality, a more fundamental perception. I call the latter primary perception to distinguish it from secondary (sense) perception. The way in which we refer to what we experience by primary perception is through what Whitehead calls symbolic expression. Symbolic expression is not something that we superimpose fictively on a set of primary qualities. Symbolic expression is the way in which we indispensably come in touch with certain dimensions of reality that can't be gotten at by the abstractive method of science.

Furthermore, science is kind of a double abstraction. First our five senses abstract from the totality of causal ingredients that are being felt by us in primary perception. Science selects from those, from the sense perceptions, certain primary qualities, things that can be easily quantified. So science is in many ways the result of a two-fold set of abstractions. This is not to indict science. This is science's proper way of focusing. To abstract means to focus in a certain way. That means you have to leave certain things out. Physics, as Holmes Rolston, III has said, is the result of a series of clever decisions about what to leave out. And I think that is somewhat true about science in general. I know that there are a lot of physicists who would deny that, but that is because they have their own kind of metaphysics, which is different from the kind of metaphysics that I am proposing here. You really have here two belief systems that are coming into encounter with each other. It is not so much science versus religion, but the clashing of two belief systems.

Scientific Separation

Saturday Afternoon

[Questioner 11] I would argue against the separation of science from other experience. Science is also driven by certain primitive concepts in our minds such as those of number, dimension, place and time that we have known since very early in life. When you say, let us leave science unto itself, we are setting aside the fact that science is already conditioned heavily by human nature. So I am wondering how it is even possible to put a boundary around or carve a domain out for science, and say we won't invade that.

[Haught] Well, I wonder how many scientists would want a view of science in which there are no boundaries, in which science sort of fades into common sense, and into our ordinary ways of interacting with the world. I think most scientists want science to be somewhat distinct from other methods of inquiry, don't they? But I understand what you are saying. Science is never pure. As Michael Polanyi has pointed out, and I agree with him completely, there is a fiduciary aspect in science. In other words there is an element of faith that the scientist has. There's an inextricably personal character to science. Science is something that is undertaken because of specific research projects. It is undertaken because it is interesting. Why is it interesting? I don't think you can answer that question scientifically. There are also all sorts of extra-scientific things, things extraneous to science, which explain psychologically, sociologically, historically, why we get interested in a particular research project.

But I am talking about method. Scientific method is different from the way in which we ordinarily eat supper. It has a history, it has an authority, it has boundaries and it has authorities who control these boundaries. Even though it is distinct from other ways of looking at the world, I would agree with you that it is not separate. I would want to distinguish between the words "distinction" and "separate." Science is really, as you say, interwoven with everything we think and everything we do. And a lot of the basis for science arises out of the nature of human consciousness and so forth. But still I want to make room for scientists to say, "When we look at this we are not going to bring in miracles, we are not going to bring in God, we are not going to appeal to spirits like we often do in the rest of life." So my idea is to not require that scientists bring things like spirits and miracles into their explanations. I would distinguish science carefully from other kinds of consciousness.

Science Without Faith

Sunday Morning

[Questioner 12] Two words came to mind during your lecture this morning. You used neither of them, so I will bring them up. I'm using a new textbook this week in my astronomy class. At the beginning of the book a distinction is made between science and religion. The claim is that science doesn't involve faith; it involves a well-defined scientific method, and religion involves faith. And in light of your talk this morning, is that a misrepresentation, is that a misnomer? If one is trying to get a multi-layered explanation, does that require more faith than a clear, distinct, abstract explanation?

[Haught] I think of how Einstein himself, who was not even a theist, would have answered. He said that there is no such thing as science acting in a void, independent of faith. There has to be faith, faith in the intelligibility of the universe. He says that is the faith that is absolutely necessary for science to get off the ground and continue working. Michael Polanyi talks about the fiduciary aspects — from the Latin word *fides* — the element of faith that sustains the scientist in his or her work. There's a personal dimension that underlies it. I understand what your textbook is saying. It wants to distinguish carefully between faith and science, and by faith it means religious faith. But the distinction is not all that clear, at least in my mind. Scientific naturalists, though, as I noted this morning, would probably be the last to realize that there is a faith system that underlies their whole worldview.

[Questioner 13] Well, what if we go to the other side? Does a multi-layered explanation take more faith or not?

[Haught] I am glad you asked the question. I think not. In fact, it does come down to a wager that we have to make between explanatory monism and explanatory pluralism as our way of approaching the real world. The explanatory monist has to have just as much faith that this particular approach, which leaves out the plurality of levels of explanation, will get us to reality more readily and more efficiently than if we invoke aesthetic and other layers of approach.

But it is also a matter of faith on my part that I would approach the universe through an explanatory pluralism, rather than monism.

However, after you make that distinction you can start asking which is the most reasonable? Which is the most likely to capture the totality of the real? I'll take my chances on explanatory pluralism. Because it tries not to leave anything out, its net is cast wide. Maybe it will bring in a lot of nonsense with it, as the naturalist would say, but at least it is an attempt to allow that there are dimensions of reality which I risk leaving out, if I approach the world through explanatory monism. Explanatory monism is the approach that Owen Flanagan advocates when he says, "Philosophy needs to make the world safe for naturalism." What he means is, let's get rid of all these traditional ways of approaching reality, all these fuzzy analogies and metaphors that religions use, and let's be very clear and distinct in our way of looking at things. However, Whitehead says that when you reduce things to the clear and distinct, you have probably left out everything fundamental.

Values in Science

Friday Evening

[Questioner 10] Do you see any values arising from either religion or science that may help to look at values in science for example? One author says that a value-altering principle is the idea of pairing. In pairing an existing value from one discipline is coupled with a similar value from another which acts as a reinforcer. The paired value becomes our new value. Do you see this resulting from the dialog between religion and science?

[Haught] I personally think that, strictly speaking, it is not the business of science to talk about values. The scientific method itself — this may not be your view of science, but this is how I've been taught science is conducted — is more concerned with understanding things in a value-free type of context. However, it's very difficult to maintain that ideal in practice, because we are persons. And, as Michael Polanyi points out, we are constantly making evaluations. Furthermore, as Einstein pointed out, it's because we value truth, honesty, and so forth, that we do science in the first place. So there is an aspect of value that underlies science.

You gave the example of pairing as a value. I think that this fits very closely to what Teilhard is saying. When you have entities that are in some sense in communion with one another, then you have something that is intrinsically more valuable than you have when those same things exist in isolation from one another. And certainly science has really intensified our awareness of that. It's doing so now especially in some developments in biology, where endosymbiosis and events like that are becoming more and more a part of our understanding of how evolution works. Evolution is not just competitive. There is a cooperative aspect to it that from a meta-scientific point of view seems to me to be an example of science discovering values that are buried in nature.

Layered Explanation

Sunday Morning

[Questioner 13] How much of a common ground is a discipline of layered explanations?

[Haught] That is a very good question. The next question, and the most difficult of all, is, how are we going to correlate one explanation with another? In the layered-explanation model we have primarily a recognition of the de-coupling of one level from the other. So what you talk about at one level does not map easily onto another. It seems to me that this is only a first step in the dialog, to get our ducks in a row, as it were. One of the big problems is conflation. Conflation occurs when creationists expect the Bible to yield scientific information. They are implicitly taking the mindset of the modern scientific world and are expecting the Bible to compete with evolutionary explanations in answering questions about the origin of life, and that sort of thing.

But conflation also takes place at the level of naturalism. It seems to me that naturalism is a conflation of science with a belief system. That is just as much a violation of the integrity of science as is creationism, although you will not find most evolutionary materialists agreeing with that. So we still have an awful lot of work to do, in terms of finding some common ground, as you put it. I think one thing we can do to start with is to address the question of where science and religion come from. Don't they have, in a sense, a kind of common origin? I think they do. They have an origin in what

Bernard Lonergan calls the pure, unrestricted desire to know. And so there is a kind of original font from which they both flow in human consciousness, which is the desire to know. But after that things get a bit messier, and a lot more difficult to correlate.

But you also have what I call the contact position. To me the paradigmatic representative of that is Teilhard de Chardin, who was able to take the results of his evolutionary understanding of the world and integrate them into a vision that had Christ at the center, yet still allowed paleontology and geology and all the other sciences that are tributary to evolution science, to have a role in building up a textured sort of view. So I would answer your question very briefly by saying, I have to use Teilhard's principle that true union differentiates. And in the science and theology discussion, we have to make sure that the two are differentiated before we can relate them. The scholastics asked why we distinguish. We distinguish not just to leave things hanging. We distinguish in order to relate. And I agree with you, this is the work that we still need to do. We need to do it again. Teilhard is not enough for today, because science has gone a lot farther than it had in his day. But it seems to me that he still provides the model for what we need to do in a contemporary situation. And we should not be afraid to somehow synthesize them. But it is a *differentiated* synthesis.

Evolution and Darwinism
    a. Dawinism and Beyond
    b. Darwinism and Access to God
    c. Evolution of God and Fidelity
    d. Evolutionary Purpose and Perfection
    e. Darwinism

Darwinism and Beyond

Saturday Morning

[Questioner 14] The topic is science and theology. But we are not talking about science. We are talking about an anthropomorphic conceptualization, which I don't think really maps on contemporary science at all. I think things such as chaos theory, astrophysics, plasma physics, and neuroscience are the most exciting in terms of possibly exploring an underlying conceptualization of God.

Are we limiting ourselves by having an anthropomorphic human explanation of God? There is a voluminous amount of information available to us that has exploded since World War II, Whitehead, and Darwin.

Evolution is not something that is within the mainstream. So are we limiting ourselves in terms of the humanistic view of God? What we are talking about is very archaic.

The best way to talk about it is in terms of corporate consulting. Corporations are much more aware of the new science and how it impacts on human interactions than a lot of the social scientists and a lot of the theologians.

[Haught] Well, you have a number of issues, and I don't know just where to start. I think our conversation this weekend has been a very limited one so far. I would agree with you that there are a lot of things that we have left out. However, when we talk, as I have this morning, about an unfinished universe, this is something that we didn't know about 150 years ago. It is science that has taught us that we live in this kind of a universe. I would disagree with you vehemently that Darwinism is passé. From what I have been able to see, Darwin is more important now than ever in the scientific community. In fact, there has been a kind of expansion of the Darwinian explanation recently, beyond the biological into the human. Darwinian algorithms are central to computational theory, and even cosmology now. Lee Smolin and others are talking about how the universe itself is a consequence of selection. The biologists I've talked to would say that the key integrating concept in the biological sciences is evolution. I don't see how evolution is anthropomorphic, or anthropocentric. I just don't quite understand you on that point.

But I do agree with you that there is room for thinking of theological issues in terms of new models that are arising from chaos theory and complexity theory — and new understandings of power itself, which we have been talking about this morning, in terms of chaos and complexity theory. I'm completely in agreement with you that we need a broad range of discussions on science and religion. I've tried to undertake this myself in my work.

You've mentioned scientific knowledge itself, the way in which scientific knowing is being discussed by philosophy of science. That certainly has an impact on the way that we construct theological method as well. So I guess in principle I have no objection to what you are saying. I guess I need to have it fleshed out a little more. Maybe some other people have some thoughts on this.

Darwinism and Access to God

Saturday Morning

[Questioner 4] Although I agree that biologists have not discarded Darwinism, I do think that it is dangerous to expand the Darwinian logic to any and every field. And we no longer see the universe as static. But there may be an intellectual pride here. Once all we knew about God came from the scriptures or tradition, and the book of nature was kind of neglected. But are we now erring in the other direction? Are we now trying to develop all of our theology based on the book of nature, on Darwinian evolution and the new physics? Where does that leave God's self-revelation to us? I think we need to strike a balance. Is God an objective reality that has something to say to us?

[Haught] To us as humans, you mean? First of all I want to agree with you that we don't want to extend the Darwinian paradigm into an absolute and ultimate explanation for everything. In fact, the point of my latest book, *Deeper than Darwin*,[3] is to say precisely that. Darwin can give us partial explanations, but ultimate explanations are beyond its prowess, its ability.

It is interesting to look historically at this whole idea of the book of nature. At one time, it was "in." In post-enlightenment England, for example, it was conventional to use the book of nature rather than the book of scripture as our primary access to God. And of course the Methodist reaction and other pietistic reactions to that are very well known. We had left something out. We had left out exactly what you said should be there. The sense of God's intimacy with us in our own personal lives had been abstracted from this intellectually appealing idea of the book of nature.

But if you go back a few centuries in the historical record, it seems, at least from what I can gather, that it was only in modern times that Christians lost touch with the natural world. In the biblical expression you find a sense of a cosmos there in the background all the time. This was not an anthropocentric world. And this idea of the cosmos being a part of theology persisted into medieval thought as well. But when the scientific revolution came about (Michael J. Buckley in his book *At the Origins of Modern Atheism*,[4] has a very good history of what happened) we tried, for a while, to make God the foundation of physics. We had put physics on a theological foundation. But then physics found it was able to provide its own foundations, after the French encyclopedists, Diderot and others. So what happened when physics was able, at least in the minds of post-enlightenment thinkers, to be its own foundation? Theology became increasingly superfluous, cosmologically speaking.

And so at the beginning of the modern period it was as though theologians said to scientists, "OK, you can have the natural world as your franchise. And we theologians will deal with things that science can't deal with, such as the human quest for meaning, spiritual life, social justice, and things like that. We will take the ultimate human questions and deal with those, and let science deal with the natural world." As a result I think theology lost touch with the natural world. And for the most part, if you look at the way in which theology is taught in our seminaries today, Catholic and non-Catholic alike, very, very few courses deal with the natural world. And this is so ironic, because the natural world is as much a part of God's creation as everything else. At seminaries there is very little of the kind of discussion that we are having today of the relevance of science to religion. As far as I know there is almost none at all. So when you talk about losing the sense of revelation, to me at least it is also good that we are moving away from the modern approach to theology, which was to forget about the natural world altogether. I think the pendulum tends to swing back and forth, and we can certainly err on the side of not talking about God's revelation to us humans. But one of the things that we have learned in the last 30 or 40 years, as a result of astrophysics as much as anything else, is that we cannot really disassociate the cosmic story from our own story.

A lot has changed since I came to Georgetown. There was a time when I was in agreement with you on the point that we have to keep the revelatory experience of God completely separate from what science is telling us about the natural world. And that is still a nice default position for us if things get complicated when we are thinking about the theological implications of science. We can always go back and say, "Well, religion and theology are talking about one set of questions, science about another. Let's keep them distinct in our own minds." But I have been increasingly unable to do that. And, like Teilhard, I just can't personally divorce my story and my own interests as a human being from the whole 30 volume preamble that I talked about last night. That is my story too. When I tell my story today, I have to include that whole cosmic story. When we tell the story of Christ today, we have to remember that every atom in the incarnate God in whom Christians believe, was forged in massive stars. That is part of His story, too. So when I talk about resurrection, as I was a while ago, it is my story entering into the divine life. Because of the inseparability of my story from the cosmic story and from the earth's story, and from the evolutionary story, it all comes along with me. To me this makes the whole notion of resurrection much more momentous than if it is just my soul or my own personal body being raised up. The whole universe is involved here.

[**Questioner 4**] But I think that in studying the natural world we should also integrate what God may have to say as well. I'm not supposing a separation, but I'm saying we should incorporate this.

[**Haught**] But, going back to those thirty volumes that I was talking about last night, when does God's revelation in history take place? It takes place in the last line of the very last page of that very last volume. So there is a temptation to leave out those other thirty volumes, and that is what I don't want to do. I want to say — and actually there are some grounds for saying this, at least in my Catholic tradition of natural theology and general revelation — that God's fundamental revelation is unfolding in the whole cosmic story. In some sense God's entering into human history is not separate from that larger story, but is continuous with it in some way. I don't want in any way to demean historical revelation. But I want to bring the whole cosmic story into that.

Evolution of God and Fidelity

Saturday Morning

[**Questioner 15**] The concept of the suffering God involves, at least in my opinion and simple understanding of process theology, some kind of an evolutionary process within the Godhead. How do you reconcile that with the concept of eternity, in which time is really not one variable at all? Also, I'm reminded of the Teilhard de Chardin quote that heaven is eternal discovery and eternal growth.

[Haught] One way to solve this problem is for me to stop talking at all. And that might be better for all of us. But, that is a very good question. Incidentally, I don't consider myself a process theologian. I use aspects of process thought, but I also use all sorts of other sources, too. Some people would say I should be sentenced to the eclectic chair. The question of how to reconcile this becoming, this changing within God, with the eternity of God is a classic chestnut for the process people. I think the best answer is given by a process thinker named Schubert Ogden, in a book called *The Reality of God and Other Essays*.[5] But others such as Charles Hartshorne and Whitehead had given a similar response before, although Whitehead did not develop his response the way theologians have.

You can have what is called a dipolar understanding of God. There are two poles to God. On the one side there is the eternity, on the other side there is the temporality. On the one side there is the immutability, unchangingness, on the other side there is the changingness or becoming of God. So the question is: how do you hold those poles together in a conceptually coherent way? It is not hard to do if you think of the eternal aspect of God religiously, and you don't want to disassociate theology from religious experience. Otherwise it becomes completely abstract and pointless. A fundamental theme in the biblical understanding of God is God's eternal fidelity. One thing that will never change about God, one thing that is always eternal, is that God will be faithful to the end. That is the religiously meaningful idea of the unchangingness of God. And precisely because God is eternally faithful, God makes the divine self vulnerable to what happens in the world. As the world changes, God's internal life changes. Otherwise we end up with a concept of God as stony immobility, a rock-like presence, which has really no religious meaning to us. So you can hold the two ideas of God's eternity and God's temporality together, if you think in terms of such ideas as the divine fidelity

A good analogy would be a mother who is perpetually faithful to her child. When the child gets in trouble, or when something happens to the child, the mother's whole emotional, affective life is completely changed by the suffering of her child. Process thought considers God in a similar way. In no way does it jeopardize the eternity, the timelessness of God. Rather it actually injects a religious meaning into those terms that the classical tradition, I think, often left out through its emphasis on the impassability, immutability, infinity and eternity of God. Literally, eternity means non-temporality. And, yes, there is a sense in which God is non-temporal. Nothing that ever happens in time is going to destroy the divine fidelity, the divine love. That's fixed. But precisely because it is fixed, it is malleable, it is adaptable, and it can change with the winds of time and history.

Your other point was about heaven as eternal discovery. By the logic of the categories of theology, the world is finite, God is infinite. So the relationship of the finite to the infinite, by definition, has to be one in which the finite always has a future. So even eschatologically, that is even in terms of our ultimate destiny, if you want to think in those terms, God is still not something that can be soaked up in one instant by virtue of the definition of "infinite." There always remains that infinite horizon that keeps receding as we approach it. So I don't think that we should necessarily think of eschatology as implying a state of final, fixed deadness, where everything comes to a static end. Rather, maybe we could even think, as some theologians do, of our final destiny as entering into an unrestricted adventure into deity. Here on earth our adventure is restricted, but eschatologically it can become an unrestricted adventure. So the future remains — even in the beyond. Karl Rahner's thought is open to that interpretation.

Evolutionary Purpose and Perfection

Saturday Afternoon

[Questioner 16] If the perfection of beauty is a direct extension of God, what is the purpose of having gone through all of this? What is the purpose of the evolutionary process?

Is the perfection of beauty a final state, or is it also a dynamic state? And if it is dynamic, what differentiates it from the here and now? Did you claim that as we progress through evolution toward that state God recedes? Could you say more about the final state of perfection?

[Haught] I mentioned that the fundamental distinction in theism is between the infinite and the finite. If that is the case even an eschatological embrace of the finite by the infinite would allow ample room for further dynamic entry into the mystery of the divine. Here I am echoing some other theologians who have talked about this. You might want to think of our eschatological condition, as human beings, as a condition in which the rather limited form of relationality, which we have to the universe now, at death becomes what Karl Rahner calls a *pancosmic* relationship. We hope that we will not be detached from this wonderful universe, but that we will be able, like God and with God, and with the communion of saints, to relate to this cosmos, to the universe and to creation, theologically speaking, more intimately and more intensely than we are able to do in our limited type of existence and freedom now.

I've also come to understand freedom in a process-relational way. Freedom means to have a capacity for relationships and not to become isolated. In some sense I believe God's freedom consists of God's absolute capacity to relate to everything intimately. So hopefully that for which we long, eschatologically, as human beings, would include a capacity to relate more intimately to everything.

Darwinism

Sunday Morning

[Questioner 17] As a biblical scholar, I have learned to be aware of some of the pitfalls of my own profession and of the misuse of the Bible. Darwinists need to be aware of the Darwin clubs of the latter 19th and early 20th century, scattered all over England, America, and Germany, that promoted the superiority of the so-called white race. The Nazis put these ideas into political action.

The Bible teaches that while there is a unity between the animal world and the world of humanity, yet humanity is something more: Humankind is made in the image of God. Humanity is too sacred and complex to be studied in our laboratories, at least without the consent of the subject, and even then, only under rigidly-controlled conditions. Hitler tried it, and we condemn him. Our biblical Jewish, Christian, and Muslim faiths are a great resource to fight this sin against humanity. Let us watch that we neither weaken nor desert our biblical faith for the false faith in a "scientific" Darwinian theology and social ethic.

I affirm the biblical stories in Genesis 1-2 as theological guides in the development of our 21st century understanding of creation today. Of course we need to know what scientists are saying about creation today. But creation doesn't end with the sixth day, the creation of humanity and the animals. It ends with the seventh day, the communion of God. I then ask, in light of your presentation this morning, whether the communion of the present day might be of God with the creation, and especially with humanity.

[Haught] I really appreciate your sensitivity to some of the pitfalls that can take place here if we take Darwinism as though it were ultimate explanation. Although I did not mention it directly, part of what I was trying to get across is that of all the scientific thinkers who are inclined toward naturalism today, I find the Darwinians the most fervent. Evolution has become ultimate explanation for many Darwinian thinkers. The main reason that I wrote *Deeper than Darwin* is to say that we need to go deeper than Darwin, but without denying that, at a certain level of explanation, we can still make room for Darwinian-evolutionary accounts of things. It is a question of which we make ultimate. The abuses that you referred to of racism, Nazism, and so forth are good warnings to us not to make any naturalistic explanations absolutely final, i. e. the deepest level of our understanding of things. It seems to me that we do run into some real problems as to how to ground our ethical life in a purely naturalistic way. I don't think it can be done effectively.

Evolution and the Soul
   a. Origin the Soul
   b. Soul of the Disabled

Origin of the Soul

Sunday Morning

[Questioner 18] I deal with students a lot who are very concerned about where the soul comes in if they allow themselves to believe in Darwinian evolution. If you believe in the evolution of primates and the evolution of humans from primates, then at some point there must have been a soul, or the capacity to know right from wrong. I think that relates to the idea of the retarded and the senile. The soul concept distinguishes humans from other animals and certainly earlier primates. How would you address this issue?

[Haught] This is something that people pointed out about the Pope's message when he talked about evolution. Scientists complained that he had the soul being introduced when the human organism came along in evolution. The soul was kind of zapped into the evolutionary process artificially and contrivedly. I think we have to look for ways of allowing the soul to emerge in its distinctness and dignity without necessarily having it appear adventitious, or ad hoc, or magical, or interruptive. One way to do that — and a lot of people don't like this because of our traditional way of thinking — is to recognize that we are not the only organisms with animating principles. As I mentioned before, the word animal itself comes from *anima*, which means soul. In Christian tradition Thomas Aquinas, for example, talks about a vegetative soul and an animal soul in a kind of Aristotelian language. Maybe that is something that could help reduce the idea that this is an interruption of the causal continuum, as it were.

Another possibility would be to recognize, as I was pointing out this morning, that information can bring about radical discontinuity within physical, evolutionary, genetic and historical continuity. Geneticists say that our genome is 99.4% similar to that of the chimpanzee. But when you get to the level of information, even the slightest differences in sequences can have a dramatic effect. As we know from writing a sentence that if we just introduce the word "not," with three letters in it, the whole meaning is changed. So at the level of information in the human genome radical qualitative changes can result from just small quantitative variations in the genome. You can still preserve something like the hierarchical discontinuities.

The notion of the soul somehow is one that came into our religious awareness when we were still thinking vertically and hierarchically. So what we have to avoid doing in the science and religion conversation, is throwing stuff out that doesn't seem *prima facie* to fit our scientific schemes of things. We have to look for theological models that preserve all the dignity of the soul that tradition talks about, without making it seem as though it is some sort of magical interruption of the way nature works. I think it's probably possible to do that, but it is going to take a lot of work. The word "soul" has a venerable tradition to it. Look at all the hymns that we sing: "My soul praises the Lord," and similar expressions. I don't think we want to drop the word "soul," any more than we want to drop the word God, but we need a new theological framework to think about it.

Soul of the Disabled

Sunday Morning

[Questioner 4] We have been cautioned against the evils of social Darwinism, which I think by now most of us recognize when we hear about it.

There is something else that concerns me, and this is a little complicated. We have talked about emergent properties and about mind, and we talked about souls. Some have suggested that what we call soul is really mind, and that mind is really a byproduct of body, of brain chemistry, and so on. That appeals to me as a biologist.

But if soul is mind and mind is a byproduct of brain chemistry, are we going to say that someone with a malfunctioning brain or a damaged brain has no soul, and then are they expendable? I worry about whole categories of people — the unborn, the retarded, and the senile — being declared officially expendable, because after all their minds don't work, and soul and humanity are a byproduct of mind. Such people don't have very good minds, so they are expendable. What is unique to the human that requires that we give respect and dignity and protection to all of these people?

[Questioner 17] My son is handicapped. And we faced the questions of how he would fit into the world and into the Church. Some even said we should not have adopted him.

The church leadership had the courage to attack this head-on. There I see compassion.

[Questioner 19] We are parents of a handicapped 16 year old. I remember taking my son to the YMCA handicapped swim. And there were children much more severely affected, who would never learn to speak or express emotion, and who would never get out of a wheelchair. Where do we locate their humanity?

[Haught] One of the things that I think we have to recognize is that that there is just as much intrinsic dignity to the people that you are talking about as there is to the rest of us. This is because the soul is a very democratic principle. It is something that we all have.

I don't know that we have to surrender that. I don't want to surrender that basic idea in an evolutionary world view. I think in some sense we can get rid of the dualism, without in any way depreciating the notion of a soul, as Hebraic thought and early Christian thought also did. In some sense there is an aspect of our being where we are deeply touched by and taken into the divine life. To me that is the soul. It is something that abides with us. It is an intrinsic part of our being. What I would only add to that is the eschatological hope-filled picture of reality, which Judaism and Christianity have given us, that in some sense our soul is a promise, just as anything in nature. What makes nature valuable, even though it perishes, is that it is the embodiment of a promise. And it is the promise that is the principle in biblical religion of the continuity of our existence, from now into the eternal. We are all promises. There is another principle here, and that is relationality. As I said before, being in the image of God is to have the capacity to relate. Your story was a wonderful story, because it shows the soul-making, not only of the person who is handicapped, but of those who are around, because they are intensifying relationality. It seems to me that somehow soul has something to do with that.

Chaos and Complexity
    a. Chaos, Birth and Creation
    b. Complexity and Cycling
    c. Terminology and Chaos

Chaos, Birth and Creation

Friday Evening

[Questioner 14] I believe that in some of Whitehead's writing he actually talks about chaos not being equivalent to suffering, but being equivalent to life, to birth, and to creation.

[Haught] It's a different sense of the term chaos, I think.

[Questioner 14] Right.

[Haught] But chaos is the halfway house between triviality and perfection. So, whenever something novel comes into any situation of order, if the order is to appropriate that novelty, it has to break down, as it were. It has to go through what Whitehead would call episodes of chaos. But that chaos is not an end in itself. It is not a value in itself. It is something that is an essential part of the path toward value. For Whitehead value consists of ordered novelty.

[Questioner 14] If, in natural law, the chaos gave redundancy, which was the inherent value, how would that be addressed within the particular context.

[Haught] You mention the redundancy. This is a favorite term in information theory. But redundancy would be more readily correlated with monotony than with chaos. And chaos would be correlated with the notion of noise in information theory. And so something truly interesting, truly novel, in terms of information theory, has to walk the razor's edge between too much redundancy, and too much noise. Somehow information theory recapitulates the whole Whiteheadian view of things, in a different sort of idiom, as it were. I think chaos would be the correlative of noise, and redundancy would be the correlative of monotony, in Whiteheadian terms. But I'm sure there's a lot more to your questions than that.

Complexity and Cycling

Friday Evening

[Questioner 20] In your talk you emphasized that all your story lines were straight with a purpose. But I see a lot of cycling going on, for example in your story line of divergence / convergence / emergence. Isn't that repetition? And of course things have to die for there to be new life.

[Haught] Well, that's a very helpful comment. I would certainly accept that qualification. I was following a Teilhardian approach, and that's comparable to what Whitehead says. When you teach, you seek simplicity, and then you mistrust it. What I was presenting here was a very, very abstract representation. But I did so in order to counter people like Stephen Jay Gould, for example, who, in his view of life, sees nothing but meandering and no directionality at all.. Teilhard saw a lot of meandering too, a lot of cycling and a lot of feedbacks and so forth and so forth. But if you consider what he did carefully, he was essentially a "seer." He emphasized "seeing" all the time in his thought. He said that if you stand back and look at the cosmos you will see that there has been net increase of over time of organized complexity. Compare primordial radiation with the human brain. Something has clearly happened here. In the cosmic process there have been a lot of blind alleys. There has indeed been a lot of recycling and cycling and so forth and so on. But the net effect is one of a gradual increase in organized complexity. And that's the main point that I would want to make.

Similarly the aim toward beauty is frustrated time and time again so that the world, as Whitehead says, starts with a dream, but reaps tragic beauty. So, realistically, the way the world works is not simple, and it would have to meet the kind of qualifications that you just made. So your question is very helpful.

Terminology and Chaos

Saturday Afternoon

[Questioner 21] I am interested in your ideas about chaos or disorder. Last night you spoke of order and disorder converging to make beauty. Complexity theory claims that order and disorder must both be present in order for a new level of organization to emerge. Those are part of what gives freedom to the creation and makes growth possible. Then you spoke about reaching a new spiritual plateau and you used the term chaos as that which you need to get past to reach a different level that you said was a new form of organization. So here you were contrasting chaos and organization sort of along a horizontal time line. Do you see these as the same sort of chaos, or do you see these as two different approaches to how we deal with these things?

[Haught] Part of that is my problem. I did not identify what I meant by the word chaos. The way Whitehead uses the term chaos is not the same as the way chaos theorists use chaos. I was talking about his view that in the process of the world's coming into being, it goes through periods of chaos, which are, as he puts it, the half-way house between triviality and perfection. By perfection he means not the synthesis of order and disorder, but the synthesis of order and novelty. When novelty comes into any situation of order, it risks being momentarily set into disorder or disarray, or chaos, in the

Whiteheadian sense, as a stage on the way to a deeper and wider integration, a wider vision, as he sometimes calls it. That is his aesthetic metaphysics, and he wants to place everything within that framework, including our talk about God and how God influences the world. God acts not simply to uphold the order, but also to disturb the order; to prevent it from lapsing permanently into monotony and triviality. That's how God acts in the human world. I was talking about that purely at a metaphysical level. I didn't really want to confuse that sense of chaos with the deterministic chaos that physicists and others talk about.

[Questioner 21] I am not talking about deterministic chaos. That is very different. In complexity theory there must be the inclusion of elements of dependability and stochastic elements in order for something new to happen. I see this, as hopefully, a different stage than what you were describing. But I wanted to get your distinctions on this because I wasn't sure where you were placing these things. I think the disorder in the Whiteheadian process, and the stochastic disorder of complexity theory are probably different.

[Haught] I would want to distinguish those two.

Love, Suffering and Power

a. Resurrection and the Body

b. Love and Suffering

c. Union Differentiates

d. Theology and Analogy

e. Freedom/Moral Evil

Resurrection and the Body

Saturday Morning

[Questioner 22] For the moment we are rooting our discussion in a distinctly Christian notion of deity. If we are going to think about divine power we then must ask how we understand the resurrection of Jesus. There, if anywhere, we have something more than merely persuasive power at work. If that is the case, then we have more than a Whiteheadian God acting. How does one understand the resurrection of Jesus in a way that is consistent with the Whiteheadian notion of divine power?

[Haught] Here I'm thinking pretty much off the top of my head, because I don't have this fully worked out either. But it seems to me that, with the concept of a vulnerable God who is compassionately experiencing every event that happens in the universe, in some way you might understand the resurrection of Jesus, and the Christian conviction that this man still lives, as the consequence of God's taking into the divine experience, this man's whole history, his whole life and his whole death, and keeping these eternally at the heart of deity. In some ways we can understand resurrection as Hans Kung, the Roman Catholic theologian understands it, as the survival of not just our body, but what our body represents, namely the accumulation of a whole story of one's life. In some sense resurrection means that our whole story is taken into the divine. In the Christian affirmation of the Christ's resurrection it is actually the vulnerability and sensitivity of the divine to this man's suffering life that preserves it eternally at the heart of deity. So Jesus truly lives eternally because of the unfailing compassion of God. After all, the New Testament says that it was God who raised Jesus from the dead. This is one way of understanding resurrection, but certainly not the only way. There are many models you could use. But from a process perspective, the resurrection would be God's taking into the divine life and approving and saving eternally what this man went through. And our own resurrection, from a Christian point of view, is one of solidarity with this event. It is the raising, or the preserving eternally, in the divine experience, this man's life and career and work and so forth. I would just add one more thing to it, which we can perhaps talk about later. It is not only our own lives, but — because of the intrinsic connectedness of our own experience to that of the whole cosmos — the whole universe that is somehow raised and preserved in the divine experience. This formulation follows from a Whiteheadian way of thinking of reality not just in terms of physical chunks of stuff, but in terms of chains of *happenings* or series of events.

Saturday Morning

[Questioner 20] I thought that your answer about the resurrection of Christ was incomplete. Jesus certainly appeared to his disciples after the resurrection. Why couldn't he have just left his body in the tomb? Why was it so important that his body disappeared?

Was that just to persuade the disciples that he had actually risen from the dead? If his body actually did disappear, can you explain that by claiming that God persuaded the molecules of his body to disperse? It seems like something more is happening there than the type of God you are trying to describe.

[Haught] Well, as I said, this is only one model and I think that we need a diversity of models. The question was how, in the framework of process thought, can we understand the resurrection? There are other frameworks, and perhaps you have another framework in mind. Many other people have other frameworks within which we can think. The resurrection itself is — and I don't want this to lead to more confusion — a metaphor as well. All of our language about divine things is symbolic and analogous. And that is consistent with what I was talking about last night. Whenever we are talking about something of ultimate significance, it grasps hold of us more than we grasp hold of it. What the disciples apparently experienced after the death of Jesus was that they were being grasped by something deep, beautiful, alive, eternal. And the way in which they expressed this experience was partly through the resurrection model. But there are other ways in which they talked about it. They talked about it in terms of Pentecostal imagery, of being enlivened by the Spirit as well. There are perhaps other ways in which theology is invited to try to give expression to this fundamental belief that Christians have that death is not the final word, that the death of Jesus is somehow introduction into a new dimension.

But because this dimension is so much larger than anything we can directly capture in objectifying language, we have to use language that is inevitably fuzzy. And theology should never apologize for using fuzzy language. This is a Whiteheadian principle too. We can be clear and distinct only by leaving out most of the reality of things. So if we find that our theology is clear and distinct, and we think that we have mastered its subject matter intellectually, then we have lost its depth. We've lost its power over us, as it were. So that is why theology — including process theology — has to be careful of thinking that it has given an absolutely clear, final, distinct, fully-wrapped-up picture of what the Christ-event signifies. So at the end of every theological discourse we should do what Job did, and that is to press our fingers to our lips, and say "This is far too much for me to talk about it. Henceforth I will live in silence." Ultimately I think good theology comes back to that theme of silence.

But then we can't be silent all the time. We have to try, we have to struggle, to represent in our conversations with one another, what this event means. So process theology is only one of many schemes that historically have been available to provide us with concepts with which to try to make sense of what is an overpowering event. So if you experience some dissatisfaction, I think that is good. It means that we have a long way to go in our conversations about this. And I think that we have to caution ourselves that we are never going to reach a conclusion that we will find satisfying intellectually and that is going to be satisfying to everybody else. What we are dealing with is simply too big for us. And that's my way of getting myself off the hook here.

Love and Suffering

Saturday Morning

[Questioner 23] God is love. Why do love and suffering always seem to go together? That is a big mystery I've always wondered about.

[Haught] I'm glad you used that word "mystery," because I don't really know. I don't know that I could articulate that conjunction conceptually. But it seems to me that what love wants is not suffering, but to conquer suffering. That is why I would hesitate to say that love and suffering are necessarily associated with each other. I am not sure that I would agree that they always have to go together. Love wants the integrity and the thriving of the other. Love wants to overcome the suffering of others. I think this is the God that Christianity, and the Bible in general, has given us.

It raises some very interesting issues. We were talking at the table this morning about Mel Gibson's new film[6], which I haven't seen. But according to what I have heard about it, suffering is portrayed in what some people think is an excessive sort of way, as almost essential to salvation. The idea is that the more you pour on suffering, somehow the more expiatory, the more effective the suffering is. I'm going to talk a little bit about suffering this morning and how I think, in ways that I can't go into right now, that the whole issue of suffering and its meaning take on a different finish or character when you place suffering in the context of an evolving universe: a universe which is still in the process of being created. Suffering in an unfinished universe has a different meaning, it seems to me, from what suffering has meant when we presumed that the universe was created perfectly and fully and integrally in the beginning, and then got messed up. When we thought that it got messed up, then a culprit, whether we ourselves or some demonic or superhuman force or whatever, messed it up. So some people, some historians, now think that this has precipitated some kind of a search for victims that we can somehow make atone for the primordial breach.

So again, I haven't seen the movie, but I wonder if Gibson's approach is not in this vein. This is quite understandable in terms of the pre-evolutionary tradition, which places suffering within what I would call an expiatory vision of existence. Wherever there is so much guilt, there has to be a proportionate amount of suffering to expiate it.

So what happens, then, if there was, as evolution implies, no historically, primordially perfect creation? And hence no primordial fault that defiled that primordial creation? What is the meaning of suffering if instead we live in a universe which is still struggling to come into being? Somehow suffering has something to do with the fact of an unfinished universe. And that changes the meaning of Christ's suffering, it seems to me in an exciting way, from just expiation to somehow participating in the creation's process of coming into being. Also — and this is the most important feature of the whole shift of horizons to an evolutionary perspective — it opens up the future in ways that the old static universe did not. And, therefore, it gives reason for hope. I think, if you look at the Genesis story of creation and what we call "the fall" that behind the scenes there is a struggling on the part of the biblical consciousness itself to shift the horizon to one of expectation rather than expiation, so that expectation becomes the horizon or the framework for our understanding suffering. It is no longer expiation. If you read the Book of Hebrews the way Gerd Theissen, a brilliant Lutheran biblical theologian reads it, the meaning of that letter is that when Christ enters into the temple once and for all (efápax), the age of expiation has passed. I find that brilliant because it also opens up the horizon of expectation, rather than expiation as the framework within which to think of suffering.

And I'm afraid that Gibson's pouring on the suffering flows more from an expiatory vision than from one of expectation. That's the sense that I get, but I shouldn't speak because I still haven't seen the movie. Those are just some thoughts that I have on this.

Saturday Morning

[Questioner 7] I think that we have undersold love when we put it only in the suffering context, just as some would argue that our God-concept gets too limited if we only talk about love and suffering. Love has many manifestations. We do not always see suffering in acts of love. Love is present in creation, and it's not suffering in that environment. Love is involved in providing, and that is a power act. Love in human life, and I would suggest also in God's relationship with the creation, has many manifestations. Suffering focuses love. Suffering is a test, if you will even, of love. But it is only one of many manifestations of love. And I think there is a danger in process thought when love and suffering are put so closely together that we forget the many other creative-power aspects of love. Suffering is a way of focusing love, but not of defining it.

[Haught] That is very nicely put. I completely agree.

Union Differentiates

Saturday Afternoon

[Questioner 3] This is on the "true union differentiates" theme. What might distinguish a true union from something else? And is there a distinction between relatedness and union? There are certain kinds of relationships that are not healthy but are abusive and repressive not allowing the other to be free.

[Haught] Well, I think we could probably all come up with examples of that. Somebody mentioned that a good marriage is one in which ideally the partners would be differentiated. One would not engulf or swallow up or dissolve the other, and the other would not allow her or himself to be engulfed. The two would become more and more differentiated. And precisely because of that, the intensity of the union is more beautiful, more magnificent and more stable. So that would be a good example of true union.

Jesus' hope is that "all may be one," and you find in Paul the idea that there are many gifts and there is much diversity. So a unity that includes and actually promotes diversity would be the ideal. And that fits into Whitehead's notion of beauty. Beauty is the harmony of contrasts. Where there is no contrast, there is harmony, but that harmony is monotonous. So, true, intense beauty, aesthetically, is one in which differentiation persists.

Theology and Analogy

Saturday Morning

[Questioner 14] What if there isn't an adventure? Perhaps it always exists, and our perceptions are not sharp. Perhaps infinity and what is finite are total illusions.

Jesus did not give us very many answers. He spoke in parables, and we interpret them. The resurrection could be a metaphor. It is not the matter that is resurrected, but the forces, which have a quantum picture. Would it be useful to utilize this to start a dialog with scientists and to allow ourselves more of a perspective, rather than forming constructs at a very early stage?

[Haught] I would say in general that it is certainly legitimate and useful for theology to use as analogy, but not literally, contemporary concepts in science. One such analogy, which I am going to talk about tomorrow, is that of information. The way in which information works in the world, is something that theology could use as an analogy for divine action. Some people that I have read have talked about resurrection as legitimated conceptually now by some of the subtleties in physics itself. I have to say I am a little bit uncomfortable theologically with doing that, partly because we are applying an analogy from the purely scientific, objective realm to talk about something which doesn't really fit into that realm. In some sense, resurrection, it seems to me, transcends the whole of contemporary understanding of the physical universe. And that is why I want to dwell on the idea that theology as such should never say "only an analogy" or "only a symbol." Analogy and symbol are actually signs that we are dealing with something momentous. So I'd be happy to use those as analogies, but I'd be very careful in my usage of them.

Freedom and Moral Evil

Saturday Afternoon

[Questioner 24] A world given freedom also has the possibility of reacting negatively to God. You haven't said very much about the presence of moral evil, and how this fits into the picture that you have given us.

[Haught] I certainly do not want to leave that out at all. I think you are exactly right that we have to make room for that, because after all, it is a fact. How does that fit into an evolutionary cosmology? My sense is that it fits in quite easily, because of the fact that we are talking about an adventure here. That is the term Whitehead uses. An adventure implies risk. There is the risk of evil not only in the sense of disorder, but there is also the risk of evil in the sense of monotony, which is the clinging to irrelevant forms of order when it is opportune, when it is time in the adventure, to move on to more intense versions of ordered novel. So there is the evil of monotony as well as the evil of disorder.

Sometimes in class when I am asked to deal with this I ask my students to think of examples of the evil of monotony. (And I am not referring to my lectures.) An example that occurs to me, a monstrous example of such a thing, is the Nazi phenomenon. What is it that is evil about Nazism? At least in part the evil consists of its exclusion of diversity; its attempt to bring about a harmoniousness which leaves out justice. I think that the theme of justice fits with the process cosmology quite nicely. Justice demands that we entertain diversity, that we bring the marginalized, those who don't belong, into the center of our social existence. Nazism and similar types of political experiments want to exclude. Racism is another form of the evil of monotony. In racism we don't want to bring diversity into our situation. Whenever diversity comes about, of course, there is the possbility of at least temporary disorder as well. So the pendulum swings back and forth between chaos and monotony.

There is plenty of room for evil in the kind of universe I have been discussing. There is not only the evil of disorder, which is pretty much what people focused on before the sense of a processive universe came into our consciousness. But now, after the cosmos has been shown to be a process, an adventure, a drama, there can be episodes of the evil of monotony as well. So, in a way there is more room for considerations of evil in this kind of universe than in the static universe of traditional philosophy. There's also room for redemption as well, but that is something that we have to hope for.

Sunday Morning

[Questioner 16] I want to go back to the first comments of this discussion. I think this was in reference to what you had said about not having a complete or perfect creation at the beginning and the fall corrupting that perfection, but rather that we have a constantly incomplete and evolving creation. I believe the real question must deal with evil and where evil enters the creation. Is evil a real force that we contend with, or is evil just a result of social evolutionary aberrations that get filtered out in the process of evolution?

[Haught] This is something that is too big for me. The notion of *adaequatio* applies just as much to our approaching the fact of evil as it does, almost, to the question of the divine. It is oftentimes people who are most sensitive and who have gone through a life experience and have experienced the monstrosity of evil, and have seen into the heart of it, to the abyss of it, to the nothingness of it, as it were, who are the most adequate to talk about it. And even they have to struggle for analogies and metaphors when they talk about it. So, by resituating creation in the context of evolution, I don't in any way want to play down the enormity of evil and the need for this world to be redeemed. My own reading of Teilhard is such that he understands the flaw that needs to be redeemed as much wider, actually, than a purely literalist interpretation of scripture would allow for. It has a cosmic quality to it. It is not just an anthropic thing, not just a human thing. It has something much larger to it. Therefore his picture of Christ, which I did not talk about, has to be proportionate to the cosmic flaw. Original sin means more than just something that is human, it is something that is already there.

All of the narratives about evil are important for us to look at since they express real sensitivity to evil. But to take them too literally, to me, is not to take them seriously. I am not sure that in my theology I have done so, but my intention is to take the problem of evil very, very seriously. So I think you are right that sometimes if we look at things in too progressive a way, we fail to take the magnitude of evil into account. I don't like to use the word progress. Teilhard used it, but he used it in a very technical sense, as increase in organized complexity. And that increase is clearly something that has taken place.

Paul Ricoeur has a wonderful treatment of evil in his book called *The Symbolism of Evil*[7]. He talks about how most pre-Christian, pre-Hebraic pictures of evil had a pronounced sense of what he called the anteriority of evil, that evil is somehow structured into the cosmos in ways that are so far beyond our own powers to address that they call out for something apocalyptic to take care of it. Even within the Adamic story, Ricoeur says, there is the figure of the serpent, so even the Bible did not do away completely with this idea of the anteriority of evil. In some sense evil is already there. According to Ricoeur the intuition of ancient tragedy is also there. There was already a flaw at the heart of reality before we came along and added our own complicity to it, as it were. The tragic vision of existence is one in which reality is broken right down the middle. The only way you can surmount evil in tragedy is by way of coming to a sense of courage in your own self, once you recognize that evil is insurmountable. That very recognition somehow saves me from evil, and I feel the courage welling up within me, and so forth. So the theme of the anteriority of evil is there in all these myths. And it hasn't completely disappeared even in the biblical vision of evil. So it seems that we can accommodate the evolutionary sense of an unfinished world to that of the anteriority of evil.

Notes

[1] Paperback: Simon and Shuster, 1967.
[2] Adequacy or competency.
[3] Perseus Publishing, 2004.
[4] Yale University Press, 1990.
[5] Southern Methodist University Press; Reprint edition, 1992.
[6] The Passion of the Christ.
[7] Beacon Press, 1969.

Index

About Pandora Press

*Pandora Press is a small, independently owned press dedicated to
making available modestly priced books that deal with Anabaptist,
Mennonite, and Believers Church topics, both historical and theological.
We welcome comments from our readers.*

Visit our full-service online Bookstore:
www.pandorapress.com

Harry Huebner, *Echoes of the Word: Theological Ethics as Rhetorical Practice* Anabaptist and Mennonite Studies Series (Kitchener: Pandora Press, 2005). Softcover, 274 pp. Includes bibliography and index. ISSN 1494-4081 ISBN 1-894710-56-8

John F. Haught, *Purpose, Evolution and the Meaning of Life,* Proceedings of the Fourth Annual Goshen Conference on Religion and Science, ed. Carl S. Helrich (Kitchener" Pandora Press, 2005). Softcover, 130 pp. Includes index. ISBN 1-894710-55-X

Gerald W. Schlabach, gen. ed., *Called Together to be Peacemakers: Report of the International Dialogue between the Catholic Church and Mennonite World Conference 1998-2003* The Bridgefolk Series (Kitchener: Pandora Press, 2005). Softcover, 77 pp. ISSN 1711-9480 ISBN 1-894710-57-6

Rodney James Sawatsky, *History and Ideology: American Mennonite Identity Definition through History* (Kitchener: Pandora Press, 2005). Softcover, 216 pp. Includes bibliography and index. ISBN 1-894710-53-3 ISSN 1494-4081

Harvey Neufeldt, Ruth Derksen Siemens and Robert Martens, eds., *First Nations and First Settlers in the Fraser Valley (1890-1960)* (Kitchener: Pandora Press, 2005). Softcover, 287 pp. Incudes bibliography and index. ISBN 1-894710-54-1

David Waltner-Toews, *The Complete Tante Tina: Mennonite Blues and Recipes* (Kitchener: Pandora Press, 2004) Softcover, 129 pp. ISBN 1-894710-52-5

John Howard Yoder, *Anabaptism and Reformation in Switzerland: An Historical and Theological Analysis of the Dialogues Between Anabaptists and Reformers* Anabaptist and Mennonite Studies Series (Kitchener: Pandora Press, 2004) Softcover, 509 pp., includes bibliography and indices. ISBN 1-894710-44-4 ISSN 1494-4081

Antje Jackelén, *The Dialogue Between Religion and Science: Challenges and Future Directions* (Kitchener: Pandora Press, 2004) Softcover, 143 pp., includes index. ISBN 1-894710-45-2

Ivan J. Kauffman, ed., *Just Policing: Mennonite-Catholic Theological Colloquium 2001-2002* The Bridgefolk Series (Kitchener: Pandora Press, 2004). Softcover, 127 pp., ISBN 1-894710-48-7.

Gerald W. Schlabach, ed., *On Baptism: Mennonite-Catholic Theological Colloquium 2001-2002* The Bridgefolk Series (Kitchener: Pandora Press, 2004). Softcover, 147 pp., ISBN 1-894710-47-9 ISSN 1711-9480.

Harvey L. Dyck, John R. Staples and John B. Toews, comp., trans. and ed. *Nestor Makhno and the Eichenfeld Massacre: A Civil War Tragedy in a Ukrainian Mennonite Village* (Kitchener: Pandora Press, 2004). Softcover, 115pp. ISBN 1-894710-46-0.

Jeffrey Wayne Taylor, *The Formation of the Primitive Baptist Movement* Studies in the Believers Church Tradition (Kitchener: Pandora Press, 2004). Softcover, 225 pp., includes bibliography and index. ISBN 1-894710-42-8 ISSN 1480-7432.

James C. Juhnke and Carol M. Hunter, *The Missing Peace: The Search for Nonviolent Alternatives in United States History* Second Expanded Edition (Kitchener: Pandora Press, 2004; co-published with Herald Press.) Softcover, 339 pp., includes index. ISBN 1-894710-46-3

Louise Hawkley and James C. Juhnke, eds., *Nonviolent America: History through the Eyes of Peace* Wedel Series 5 (North Newton: Bethel College, 2004, co-published with Pandora Press) Softcover, 269 pp., includes index. ISBN 1-889239-02-X

Karl Koop, *Anabaptist-Mennonite Confessions of Faith: the Development of a Tradition* (Kitchener: Pandora Press, 2004; co-published with Herald Press) Softcover, 178 pp., includes index. ISBN 1-894710-32-0

Lucille Marr, *The Transforming Power of a Century: Mennonite Central Committee and its Evolution in Ontario* (Kitchener: Pandora Press, 2003). Softcover, 390 pp., includes bibliography and index, ISBN 1-894710-41-x.

Erica Janzen, *Six Sugar Beets, Five Bitter Years* (Kitchener: Pandora Press, 2003). Softcover, 186 pp., ISBN 1-894710-37-1.

T. D. Regehr, *Faith Life and Witness in the Northwest, 1903-2003: Centenninal History of the Northwest Mennonite Conference* (Kitchener: Pandora Press, 2003). Softcover, 524 pp., includes index, ISBN 1-894710-39-8.

John A. Lapp and C. Arnold Snyder, gen.eds., *A Global Mennonite History. Volume One: Africa* (Kitchener: Pandora Press, 2003). Softcover, 320 pp., includes indexes, ISBN 1-894710-38-x.

George F. R. Ellis, *A Universe of Ethics Morality and Hope: Proceedings from the Second Annual Goshen Conference on Religion and Science* (Kitchener: Pandora Press, 2003; co-published with Herald Press.) Softcover, 148 pp. ISBN 1-894710-36-3

Donald Martin, *Old Order Mennonites of Ontario: Gelassenheit, Discipleship, Brotherhood* (Kitchener: Pandora Press, 2003; co-published with Herald Press.) Softcover, 381 pp., includes index. ISBN 1-894710-33-9

Mary A. Schiedel, *Pioneers in Ministry: Women Pastors in Ontario Mennonite Churches, 1973-2003* (Kitchener: Pandora Press, 2003) Softcover, 204 pp., ISBN 1-894710-35-5

Harry Loewen, ed., *Shepherds, Servants and Prophets* (Kitchener: Pandora Press, 2003; co-published with Herald Press) Softcover, 446 pp., ISBN 1-894710-35-5

Robert A. Riall, trans., Galen A. Peters, ed., *The Earliest Hymns of the Ausbund: Some Beautiful Christian Songs Composed and Sung in the Prison at Passau, Published 1564* (Kitchener: Pandora Press, 2003; co-published with Herald Press) Softcover, 468 pp., includes bibliography and index. ISBN 1-894710-34-7.

John A. Harder, *From Kleefeld With Love* (Kitchener: Pandora Press, 2003; co-published with Herald Press) Softcover, 198 pp. ISBN 1-894710-28-2

John F. Peters, *The Plain People: A Glimpse at Life Among the Old Order Mennonites of Ontario* (Kitchener: Pandora Press, 2003; co-published with Herald Press) Softcover, 54 pp. ISBN 1-894710-26-6

Robert S. Kreider, *My Early Years: An Autobiography* (Kitchener: Pandora Press, 2002; co-published with Herald Press) Softcover, 600 pp., index ISBN 1-894710-23-1

Helen Martens, *Hutterite Songs* (Kitchener: Pandora Press, 2002; co-published with Herald Press) Softcover, xxii, 328 pp. ISBN 1-894710-24-X

C. Arnold Snyder and Galen A. Peters, eds., *Reading the Anabaptist Bible: Reflections for Every Day of the Year* introduction by Arthur Paul Boers (Kitchener: Pandora Press, 2002; co-published with Herald Press.) Softcover, 415 pp. ISBN 1-894710-25-8

C. Arnold Snyder, ed., *Commoners and Community: Essays in Honour of Werner O. Packull* (Kitchener: Pandora Press, 2002; co-published with Herald Press.) Softcover, 324 pp. ISBN 1-894710-27-4

James O. Lehman, *Mennonite Tent Revivals: Howard Hammer and Myron Augsburger, 1952-1962* (Kitchener: Pandora Press, 2002; co-published with Herald Press) Softcover, xxiv, 318 pp. ISBN 1-894710-22-3

Lawrence Klippenstein and Jacob Dick, *Mennonite Alternative Service in Russia* (Kitchener: Pandora Press, 2002; co-published with Herald Press) Softcover, viii, 163 pp. ISBN 1-894710-21-5

Nancey Murphy, *Religion and Science* (Kitchener: Pandora Press, 2002; co-published with Herald Press) Softcover, 126 pp. ISBN 1-894710-20-7

Biblical Concordance of the Swiss Brethren, 1540. Trans. Gilbert Fast and Galen Peters; bib. intro. Joe Springer; ed. C. Arnold Snyder (Kitchener: Pandora Press, 2001; co-published with Herald Press) Softcover, lv, 227pp. ISBN 1-894710-16-9

Orland Gingerich, *The Amish of Canada* (Kitchener: Pandora Press, 2001; co-published with Herald Press.) Softcover, 244 pp., includes index. ISBN 1-894710-19-3

M. Darrol Bryant, *Religion in a New Key* (Kitchener: Pandora Press, 2001) Softcover, 136 pp., includes bib. refs. ISBN 1-894710- 18-5

Trans. Walter Klaassen, Frank Friesen, Werner O. Packull, ed. C. Arnold Snyder, *Sources of South German/Austrian Anabaptism* (Kitchener: Pandora Press, 2001; co-published with Herald Press.) Softcover, 430 pp. includes indexes. ISBN 1-894710-15-0

Pedro A. Sandín Fremaint y Pablo A. Jimémez, *Palabras Duras: Homilías* (Kitchener: Pandora Press, 2001). Softcover, 121 pp., ISBN 1-894710-17-7

Ruth Elizabeth Mooney, *Manual Para Crear Materiales de Educación Cristiana* (Kitchener: Pandora Press, 2001). Softcover, 206 pp., ISBN 1-894710-12-6

Esther and Malcolm Wenger, poetry by Ann Wenger, *Healing the Wounds* (Kitchener: Pandora Press, 2001; co-pub. with Herald Press). Softcover, 210 pp. ISBN 1-894710-09-6.

Otto H. Selles and Geraldine Selles-Ysselstein, *New Songs* (Kitchener: Pandora Press, 2001). Poetry and relief prints, 90pp. ISBN 1-894719-14-2

Pedro A. Sandín Fremaint, *Cuentos y Encuentros: Hacia una Educación Transformadora* (Kitchener: Pandora Press, 2001). Softcover 163 pp ISBN 1-894710-08-8.

A. James Reimer, *Mennonites and Classical Theology: Dogmatic Foundations for Christian Ethics* (Kitchener: Pandora Press, 2001; co-published with Herald Press) Softcover, 650pp. ISBN 0-9685543-7-7

Walter Klaassen, *Anabaptism: Neither Catholic nor Protestant*, 3rd ed (Kitchener: Pandora Press, 2001; co-pub. Herald Press) Softcover, 122pp. ISBN 1-894710-01-0

Dale Schrag & James Juhnke, eds., *Anabaptist Visions for the new Millennium: A search for identity* (Kitchener: Pandora Press, 2000; co-published with Herald Press) Softcover, 242 pp. ISBN 1-894710-00-2

Harry Loewen, ed., *Road to Freedom: Mennonites Escape the Land of Suffering* (Kitchener: Pandora Press, 2000; co-published with Herald Press) Hardcover, large format, 302pp. ISBN 0-9685543-5-0

Alan Kreider and Stuart Murray, eds., *Coming Home: Stories of Anabaptists in Britain and Ireland* (Kitchener: Pandora Press, 2000; co-published with Herald Press) Softcover, 220pp. ISBN 0-9685543-6-9

Edna Schroeder Thiessen and Angela Showalter, *A Life Displaced: A Mennonite Woman's Flight from War-Torn Poland* (Kitchener: Pandora Press, 2000; co-published with Herald Press) Softcover, xii, 218pp. ISBN 0-9685543-2-6

Stuart Murray, *Biblical Interpretation in the Anabaptist Tradition,* Studies in the Believers Tradition (Kitchener: Pandora Press, 2000; co-published with Herald Press) Softcover, 310pp. ISBN 0-9685543-3-4 ISSN 1480-7432.

Loren L. Johns, ed. *Apocalypticism and Millennialism,* Studies in the Believers Church Tradition (Kitchener: Pandora Press, 2000; co-published with Herald Press) Softcover, 419pp; Scripture and name indeces ISBN 0-9683462-9-4 ISSN 1480-7432

Later Writings by Pilgram Marpeck and his Circle. Volume 1: The Exposé, A Dialogue and Marpeck's Response to Caspar Schwenckfeld. Trans. Walter Klaassen, Werner Packull, and John Rempel (Kitchener: Pandora Press, 1999; co-published with Herald Press) Softcover, 157pp. ISBN 0-9683462-6-X

John Driver, *Radical Faith. An Alternative History of the Christian Church,* edited by Carrie Snyder. Kitchener: Pandora Press, 1999; co-published with Herald Press) Softcover, 334pp. ISBN 0-9683462-8-6

C. Arnold Snyder, *From Anabaptist Seed. The Historical Core of Anabaptist-Related Identity* (Kitchener: Pandora Press, 1999; co-published with Herald Press) Softcover, 53pp.; discussion questions. ISBN 0-9685543-0-X
Also available in Spanish translation: *De Semilla Anabautista*, from Pandora Press only.

John D. Thiesen, *Mennonite and Nazi? Attitudes Among Mennonite Colonists in Latin America, 1933-1945* (Kitchener: Pandora Press, 1999; co-published with Herald Press) Softcover, 330pp., 2 maps, 24 b/w illustrations, bibliography, index. ISBN 0-9683462-5-1

Lifting the Veil, a translation of *Aus meinem Leben: Erinnerungen von J.H. Janzen*. Ed. by Leonard Friesen; trans. by Walter Klaassen (Kitchener: Pandora Press, 1998; co-pub. with Herald Press). Softcover, 128pp.; 4pp. of illustrations. ISBN 0-9683462-1-9

Leonard Gross, *The Golden Years of the Hutterites*, rev. ed. (Kitchener: Pandora Press, 1998; co-pub. with Herald Press). Softcover, 280pp., index. ISBN 0-9683462-3-5

William H. Brackney, ed., *The Believers Church: A Voluntary Church*, Studies in the Believers Church Tradition (Kitchener: Pandora Press, 1998; co-published with Herald Press). Softcover, viii, 237pp., index. ISBN 0-9683462-0-0 ISSN 1480-7432.

An Annotated Hutterite Bibliography, compiled by Maria H. Krisztinkovich, ed. by Peter C. Erb (Kitchener: Pandora Press, 1998). (Ca. 2,700 entries) 312pp., softcover, electronic, or both. ISBN (paper) 0-9698762-8-9/(disk) 0-9698762-9-7

Jacobus ten Doornkaat Koolman, *Dirk Philips. Friend and Colleague of Menno Simons*, trans. W. E. Keeney, ed. C. A. Snyder (Kitchener: Pandora Press, 1998; co-published with Herald Press). Softcover, xviii, 236pp., index. ISBN: 0-9698762-3-8

Sarah Dyck, ed./tr., *The Silence Echoes: Memoirs of Trauma & Tears* (Kitchener: Pandora Press, 1997; co-published with Herald Press). Softcover, xii, 236pp., 2 maps. ISBN: 0-9698762-7-0

Wes Harrison, *Andreas Ehrenpreis and Hutterite Faith and Practice* (Kitchener: Pandora Press, 1997; co-published with Herald Press). Softcover, xxiv, 274pp., 2 maps, index. ISBN 0-9698762-6-2

C. Arnold Snyder, *Anabaptist History and Theology: Revised Student Edition* (Kitchener: Pandora Press, 1997; co-pub. Herald Press). Softcover, xiv, 466pp., 7 maps, 28 illustrations, index, bibliography. ISBN 0-9698762-5-4

Nancey Murphy, *Reconciling Theology and Science: A Radical Reformation Perspective* (Kitchener, Ont.: Pandora Press, 1997; co-pub. Herald Press). Softcover, x, 103pp., index. ISBN 0-9698762-4-6

C. Arnold Snyder and Linda A. Huebert Hecht, eds, *Profiles of Anabaptist Women: Sixteenth Century Reforming Pioneers* (Waterloo, Ont.: Wilfrid Laurier University Press, 1996). Softcover, xxii, 442pp. ISBN: 0-88920-277-X

The Limits of Perfection: A Conversation with J. Lawrence Burkholder 2nd ed., with a new epilogue by J. Lawrence Burkholder, Rodney Sawatsky and Scott Holland, eds. (Kitchener: Pandora Press, 1996). Softcover, x, 154pp. ISBN 0-9698762-2-X

C. Arnold Snyder, *Anabaptist History and Theology: An Introduction* (Kitchener: Pandora Press, 1995). ISBN 0-9698762-0-3 Softcover, x, 434pp., 6 maps, 29 illustrations, index, bibliography.

Pandora Press

33 Kent Avenue Kitchener, ON N2G 3R2

Tel.: (519) 578-2381 / Fax: (519) 578-1826

E-mail: info@pandorapress.com

Web site: www.pandorapress.com